Palgrave Socio-Legal Studies

Series Editor
Dave Cowan, School of Law, University of Cardiff, Cardiff, UK

Editorial Board
Dame Hazel Genn, University College London, London, UK
Fiona Haines, School of Social & Political Sciences, University of Melbourne, Melbourne, VIC, Australia
Herbert Kritzer, University of Minnesota, Minneapolis, MN, USA
Linda Mulcahy, Centre for Socio-Legal Studies, University of Oxford, Oxford, UK
Rosemary Hunter, Kent Law School, University of Kent, Canterbury, UK
Carl Stychin, Institute of Advanced Legal Studies, University of London, London, UK
Mariana Valverde, Centre for Criminology & Socio-Legal Studies, University of Toronto, Toronto, ON, Canada
Sally Wheeler, College of Law, Australian National University, Canberra, ACT, Australia
Senthorun Raj, Manchester Metropolitan University, Manchester, Lancashire, UK

The Palgrave Socio-Legal Studies series is a developing series of monographs and textbooks featuring cutting edge work which, in the best tradition of socio-legal studies, reach out to a wide international audience.

Jonathan Miaz · Evelyne Schmid ·
Matthieu Niederhauser · Constance Kaempfer ·
Martino Maggetti

Engaging with Human Rights

How Subnational Actors use Human Rights Treaties
in Policy Processes

Jonathan Miaz, Evelyne Schmid (Jonathan Miaz and Evelyne Schmid sharing first authorship), Matthieu Niederhauser, Constance Kaempfer, Martino Maggetti

Jonathan Miaz
Institute of Political Studies
University of Lausanne
Lausanne, Switzerland

Matthieu Niederhauser
Institute of Political Studies
University of Lausanne
Lausanne, Switzerland

Martino Maggetti
Institute of Political Studies
University of Lausanne
Lausanne, Switzerland

Evelyne Schmid
Centre of Comparative, European
and International Law
University of Lausanne
Lausanne, Switzerland

Constance Kaempfer
Directorate of International Law
Federal Department of Foreign Affairs
Berne, Switzerland

ISSN 2947-9274 ISSN 2947-9282 (electronic)
Palgrave Socio-Legal Studies
ISBN 978-3-031-53517-8 ISBN 978-3-031-53518-5 (eBook)
https://doi.org/10.1007/978-3-031-53518-5

Published with the support of the Swiss National Science Foundation

© The Editor(s) (if applicable) and The Author(s) 2024. This book is an open access publication.

Open Access This book is licensed under the terms of the Creative Commons Attribution 4.0 International License (http://creativecommons.org/licenses/by/4.0/), which permits use, sharing, adaptation, distribution and reproduction in any medium or format, as long as you give appropriate credit to the original author(s) and the source, provide a link to the Creative Commons license and indicate if changes were made.
The images or other third party material in this book are included in the book's Creative Commons license, unless indicated otherwise in a credit line to the material. If material is not included in the book's Creative Commons license and your intended use is not permitted by statutory regulation or exceeds the permitted use, you will need to obtain permission directly from the copyright holder.
The use of general descriptive names, registered names, trademarks, service marks, etc. in this publication does not imply, even in the absence of a specific statement, that such names are exempt from the relevant protective laws and regulations and therefore free for general use.
The publisher, the authors and the editors are safe to assume that the advice and information in this book are believed to be true and accurate at the date of publication. Neither the publisher nor the authors or the editors give a warranty, expressed or implied, with respect to the material contained herein or for any errors or omissions that may have been made. The publisher remains neutral with regard to jurisdictional claims in published maps and institutional affiliations.

Cover credit: © Melisa Hasan

This Palgrave Macmillan imprint is published by the registered company Springer Nature Switzerland AG
The registered company address is: Gewerbestrasse 11, 6330 Cham, Switzerland

Paper in this product is recyclable.

Acknowledgements

This book was written in the context of the Research Project 'Bypassing the Nation State? How Swiss Cantonal Parliaments Deal with International Obligations: International Law and Subnational Parliaments (ILSP)' at the University of Lausanne between 2019 and 2024, co-directed by Evelyne Schmid and Martino Maggetti.

We are a team of five researchers based at the University of Lausanne. Jonathan Miaz and Evelyne Schmid share co-first authorship for this book for which all five people invested time, thought and energy. We want to emphasise the collective dimension of this book and we encourage readers to list all five names (rather than 'et al.'), where possible when they cite our work. Author contributions are as follows:

Book conceptualisation: E. S., J. M., M. M., M. N., C. K.; data collection: J. M., M. N., C. K.; data analysis: J. M., M. N., C. K, M. M.; writing original draft chapters: J. M., M. N., C. K, E. S., M. M; review and editing of chapters: M. N., C. K., E. S., J. M., M. M.; book project management and corresponding author: E. S.

We would like to express our deepest gratitude to the Swiss National Science Foundation for the generous funding of this project (grant 182148). Thanks to the generous support of the Swiss National Science Foundation, we were able to build a team and gather the data to better understand the empirics of international human rights treaties at the subnational level. We are also very grateful to the University of Lausanne and in particular to the Faculty of Law, Criminal Sciences and Public Administration who provided extra financial support to catch up after the need to reschedule field work during the COVID pandemic. We would like to thank all our interview partners, who very generously volunteered their time to answer our numerous questions despite having busy schedules and the rescheduling of interviews due to the pandemic.

We would also like to thank Eva Maria Belser, Sandra Egli, Delilah von Streng and Franziska Landolt-Brändle of the Swiss Institute of Federalism with whom we organised a public event. We are also thankful to all the participants of the public conference we co-organised in November 2022 in Bern, where we could obtain the valuable feedback of members of cantonal governments, parliamentarians, human rights practitioners, and individuals most directly concerned by human rights implementation questions which we examined in the two case studies.

We particularly appreciated the help and encouragement of Alice Donald and Anne-Katrin Speck. Alice Donald hosted Constance Kaempfer in Middlesex and Anne-Katrin Speck visited us in Lausanne, both providing valuable feedback during the early stages of this project. Other project partners included Andreas Müller, Ioannis Papadopoulos, Matthew Saul, Philipp Trein, Andrea Pilotti, Simone Wegmann and Michael Zürn. Furthermore, we wish to thank all the participants at our first workshop in January 2021 for their rich input, which enabled us to acquire feedback on our ideas and to push the project forward: Eva Maria Belser, Alice Donald, Thomas Malang, Sean Müller, Yannis Papadopoulos, Anna Petrig, Matthew Saul, Arjan Schakel, Michael Tatham, Philip Trein and Simone Wegmann. Without Markus Schefer's support and mentorship nearly ten years ago, this entire multi-year project would not have seen the light of the day. Judith Wyttenbach provided continuous encouragement and her 2017 monograph on federalism an indispensable reference point.

We are also very grateful to David Coen and Tom Pegram, who hosted Matthieu Niederhauser for a research stay at the Global Governance Institute, University College London, where one of the chapters of this book was first drafted.

We are particularly grateful to the Palgrave editors and staff, especially Dave Cowan, Professor of Law and Policy, University of Bristol (editor of the Palgrave Socio-Legal Studies Series), Josephine Taylor and Abarna Antonyraj. The constructive and detailed feedback we received on our book proposal has made this book stronger and we very much appreciated the helpful and friendly scientific exchanges.

Some of the work in this project draws on the article 'From international law to subnational practices: How intermediaries translate the Istanbul Convention', published in Regulation & Governance, on Constance Kaempfer's PhD thesis (Kaempfer, 2023), as well as Matthieu Niederhauser's ongoing PhD work.

We are indebted to Robin Bindith, Mathias Délétroz, Andreia Dinis Pinto and Nadja Senn, who transcribed numerous interviews. A special thanks goes to Jill McAllister for efficiently proofreading our manuscript, and to Daniela

Serraca Fraccalvieri and Marzia Gavillet for their administrative support of the project.

Finally, we are thankful to our friends and family for their support—two babies were born during the final stages of the book-writing process! One of them helped to finish a PhD thesis, which in turn influenced a chapter of this book, and the other one pushed us to advance quickly with the drafting but then still gave us some time for rich interdisciplinary debates on the key notions of our work.

Contents

1. **The Importance of Subnational Engagement with Human Rights Treaties** — 1
   - 1.1 Introduction — 2
   - 1.2 What Readers Can Expect from This Book — 3
   - 1.3 Key Terms: Subnational Political Authorities' Engagement with Human Rights Treaties — 11
   - 1.4 Why Focus on Engagement, Rather than Compliance or Implementation? — 13
   - 1.5 Organisation of the Book — 16
   - References — 19

2. **Designing Research for Studying How Subnational Actors Use International Human Rights Treaties** — 23
   - 2.1 Restating the Research Objectives — 23
   - 2.2 Identifying the Engagement of Subnational Actors with Human Rights Treaties: An Interdisciplinary Endeavour — 25
   - 2.3 Selecting the International Treaties — 29
   - 2.4 The Collected Datasets — 36
   - References — 41

3. **Shaping the Uses of a Treaty Through Ratification and Implementation Procedures** — 47
   - 3.1 Introduction — 47
   - 3.2 Theoretical Framework on Ratification and Implementation — 48
   - 3.3 Ratification and Implementation of International Treaties in Switzerland — 51
   - 3.4 Ratification and Implementation of the Istanbul Convention — 53
   - 3.5 Ratification and Implementation of the Convention on the Rights of Persons with Disabilities — 58

	3.6 Discussion	62
	3.7 Conclusion	64
	References	65
4	**Varieties of How Actors Use Human Rights Treaties in Subnational Policy Processes**	67
	4.1 Introduction	68
	4.2 Using Treaties for Agenda-Setting	71
	4.3 Using International Treaties to Support Claims	76
	4.4 Discussion and Conclusion	82
	References	85
5	**The Different Ways in Which Subnational Political Authorities Engage with International Human Rights Treaties**	89
	5.1 Introduction	90
	5.2 Patterns of Engagement	91
	5.3 Comparative Outlook and Conditions for Engagement	109
	5.4 Conclusion	113
	References	116
6	**Towards a Contextualised Understanding of Human Rights Treaty Implementation**	119
	6.1 Taking Stock	119
	6.2 Main Implications	124
	6.3 Looking Forward	126
	References	127
Index		131

About the Authors

Jonathan Miaz is a lecturer and researcher at the Institute of Political Studies of the University of Lausanne. He holds a PhD in political science from the University of Lausanne and the University of Strasbourg. He conducted his postdoctoral research at the University of Chicago, at the American Bar Foundation, at Sciences Po Paris, at the University of Neuchâtel and at the University of Lausanne. His research interests are oriented towards the relationship between law, politics and society, street-level organisations and asylum policies. He is the author of numerous publications in the Journal of Comparative Policy Analysis: Research and Practice, Regulation & Governance, Administration & Society, Journal of Immigrant and Refugee Studies, European Policy Analysis, Droit & Société, and Politique & Société.

Evelyne Schmid is a professor in public international law at the Faculty of Law, Criminal Sciences and Public Administration of the University of Lausanne. Her main research focus is currently on positive obligations in international law and the international responsibility of states for omission. She holds a PhD from the Geneva Graduate Institute of International and Development Studies (IHEID) and was previously based at the University of Basel (Switzerland) and at Bangor University (Wales, UK). She is the author of 'Taking Economic, Social and Cultural Rights Seriously in International Criminal Law' (Cambridge Studies in International and Comparative Law, 2015; Christiane-Rajewsky award 2016) and was Vice-President of the European Society of International Law. www.ius-gentium.ch

Matthieu Niederhauser is a doctoral researcher at the Institute of Political Studies (IEP) of the University of Lausanne and was a visiting researcher at University College London. He is writing a thesis on how cantonal and inter-cantonal actors use and implement international law in Switzerland. He previously worked for the Swiss Federal Department of Foreign Affairs and for the International Committee of the Red Cross (ICRC). He recently published the following article: 'Governmental human rights focal points in federal contexts: The implementation of the Istanbul Convention in Switzerland as a case study'. Netherlands Quarterly of Human Rights (2021): 140.

Constance Kaempfer works at the Directorate of International Law of the Federal Department of Foreign Affairs of Switzerland. She was previously a senior researcher at the Centre for Comparative, European and International Law (CDCEI) at the University of Lausanne. She defended a PhD thesis on the mechanisms of implementation of international law by the Swiss cantons and her work was published *open access* in July 2023: 'Les mécanismes de mise en œuvre du droit international par les cantons suisses: études de cas dans les domaines des droits humains et des accords bilatéraux Suisse-UE'. Sui generis. Constance Kaempfer is also a licensed lawyer and authored several articles.

Martino Maggetti is an associate professor of political science at the Institute of Political Studies (IEP) of the University of Lausanne, Switzerland, where he conducted his PhD. He was previously based at the University of Zurich and has been a visiting researcher at the University of Exeter, University College London, Oxford and Antwerp. His research interests are oriented towards regulatory governance and comparative public policy. He is the author of more than 47 scientific articles, two books, and has edited a number of volumes and special issues. More information is available at: www.maggetti.org.

Abbreviations

BFEG	Bureau fédéral de l'égalité entre femmes et hommes (Federal Office for Gender Equality)
BFEH	Bureau fédéral de l'égalité pour les personnes handicapées (Federal Office for the Equality of Persons with Disabilities)
CEDAW	United Nations Convention on the Elimination of all Forms of Discrimination against Women
CRPD	Convention on the Rights of Persons with Disabilities
CSO	Civil Society Organisation
CSVD	Conférence Suisse contre la Violence Domestique (Swiss Conference against Domestic Violence)
GREVIO	Group of Experts on Action against Violence against Women and Domestic Violence (Council of Europe)
IC or Istanbul Convention	Istanbul Convention (Council of Europe Convention on Preventing and Combating Violence against Women and Domestic Violence)
MP	Member of Parliament
NGO	Non-governmental Organisation
SP	Social Democratic Party of Switzerland
UN	United Nations
UNCERD	UN Convention on the Elimination of Racial Discrimination

List of Tables

Table 2.1	Characteristics of Swiss cantons (at time of data collection) and cantons included in desk research	37
Table 4.1	Variety of uses of human rights treaties (summary)	84
Table 5.1	Different types of engagement with human rights treaties	114

CHAPTER 1

The Importance of Subnational Engagement with Human Rights Treaties

Abstract Making human rights a reality requires that various types of domestic actors take measures, which is very demanding, all the more so in federal systems. Based on a comparative case study of Swiss cantons, we argue that an important part of the game is played at the subnational level, and not following a top-down trajectory, but with repeated back and forth between and within the levels of governance. Actors use human rights treaties in the policy process, sometimes leading to an engagement that increases human rights implementation, and at other times not. In this chapter, we first explore how international law continues to rely upon states' domestic political institutions to fulfil international obligations—particularly those obligations that require the adoption of policy measures. We review how this state of affairs points to the central role of domestic actors participating in policy processes at the subnational level. Secondly, we contribute to concept formation, by explaining what we mean by political authorities' 'engagement with human rights treaties', which is a key notion that we will use to describe an often crucial, intermediary condition between inaction and the potential implementation of the treaty.

Keywords Federalism · Human rights treaties · International law's turn to the local · Parliaments · Subnational Actors and Legislators

1.1 Introduction

Human rights aim to make lives safer and freer—freer 'from fear' and 'from want' (Roosevelt, 1941). All states have accepted a plethora of human rights obligations 'to secure their universal and effective recognition and observance' (Universal Declaration of Human Rights, 1948 preamble). Yet, human rights implementation within domestic legal systems is far from automatic, let alone in federal systems, where turning rights into practice requires the presence of committed actors at all levels of the state. What is more, subnational actors in federated entities are likely to enjoy considerable room for manoeuvre in implementation, allowing them to use international human rights strategically in their policy processes.

This book is motivated by the observation that the challenges and opportunities at the intersection of international obligations and domestic legal realities are particularly acute with respect to processes located at the subnational level of federal states. We present data about how subnational actors use international human rights treaties and what the implications for the engagement of subnational political authorities are. Our research allowed us to identify the variety of uses and patterns of engagement with international human rights treaties. In this book, we explain how the uses of human rights treaties and subnational authorities' engagement with international human rights treaties play out in two case studies and how the engagement of subnational political authorities often provides a useful starting point for legislative and concrete implementation. In short, this is a book about the role of human rights treaties in subnational policy processes in a world increasingly regulated by international law.

We will show that human rights treaties can constitute a political resource for actors at the subnational level. International treaties serve as a political argument for justifying legislative reforms and institutionalising or strengthening a given public policy. We will demonstrate how human rights treaties can be used as legal resources to legitimise the authority of an administration in steering public policy and as cognitive resources for rethinking a public issue, redefining a public policy and the measures to be adopted. Our data reveals how subnational actors use human rights on the ground in subnational policy-making processes and how individual persons can play a role in increasing the engagement of political authorities with an international treaty, and in turn in facilitating stronger implementation.

We take an interdisciplinary analytical perspective, based on international and constitutional law, political science, and the sociology of law, according to which we undertook in-depth case studies at the subnational level in Switzerland through a combination of desk research and over 65 semi-structured interviews with bureaucrats, politicians, civil society actors on two international human rights treaties—the Council of Europe Convention on Preventing and Combating Violence against Women and Domestic Violence, better known as the Istanbul Convention; and the United Nations (UN) Convention on the Rights of Persons with Disabilities (CRPD)—in Swiss subnational jurisdictions.

1.2 What Readers Can Expect from This Book

This is a book about how domestic actors, and namely subnational ones, use, i.e. invoke, understand, contest or incorporate international human rights treaties and obligations into their work, and about what this means for the engagement of the subnational political authorities with human rights treaties. Based on empirical evidence from the Swiss case, we answer two related research questions:

We first ask: **How do subnational actors *use* international human rights treaties that require the adoption of measures implying the active involvement of political authorities (such as subnational parliaments and governments)?**

To answer this question, we begin by analysing how federal, inter-cantonal and cantonal actors attempt to orient the ways in which subnational actors will later use the treaties containing obligations within their domains of competence. To do so, they employ the (pre-)ratification procedure and various formal and informal implementation mechanism. This is a top-down perspective. Bottom-up processes unfold simultaneously. We are, therefore, at the same time interested in how subnational actors (such as members of cantonal parliaments, bureaucrats, civil society organisations or academic experts) use human rights treaties or parts thereof.

In this study, the use of a treaty is an instance in which a subnational actor strategically or instrumentally refers to a treaty and/or works with the treaty, e.g. by citing it or by relying on the treaty in a parliamentary speech, a draft law, a report or a discussion. Some scholars use the term 'mobilisation' of (or around) treaty commitments (Gurowitz, 1999; Simmons, 2012). For reasons of simplicity and because mobilisation is understood differently by certain scholars and practitioners, we refer to 'use' to encompass all forms of practice in which a treaty is explicitly considered by a subnational actor. A use of a treaty can sometimes lead to another use by another actor, creating an incremental and sometimes self-reinforcing process. Some actors use treaties with the explicit aim to encourage the implementation, while others use a treaty or parts of it to strategically support thematic agendas, such as the protection of persons with disabilities or gender equality. Our data shows that subnational actors use human rights treaties in iterative, incremental dynamics that play out in interdependent top-down and bottom-up paths. Subnational actors strategically consider the resources, opportunities and tools a treaty provides, build their own understanding of the obligations, interpret, appropriate, sometimes strategically refer to obligations contained in human rights treaties and occasionally contribute to the translation of obligations into concrete policy measures. Studying the uses of a treaty allows us to capture what subnational actors involved in policy processes *do* with treaties. Uses are thus a form of law in action (as opposed to law in books) in the sense that uses of international law refer to what actors actually do with a treaty. Yet, even where numerous subnational actors use treaties or parts of them, this does not yet mean that the treaties will be implemented.

For our second question, we are interested in exploring **how the various uses of human rights treaties by subnational actors shape the political authorities'** *engagement* **with international human rights treaty obligations.**

In order to implement human rights treaties at the subnational level and ensure that they play out the intended positive roles in people's everyday lives, subnational authorities in almost all cases need to actively take steps, such as adopt or modify cantonal laws, pass budgets, make information available, allocate human resources, change administrative procedures or set up institutional and organisational structures. When we refer to subnational political authorities, we refer to subnational executives and legislative bodies, i.e. actors holding institutional positions of power and formal influence within the system of governance.[1] For our second research question, we ask whether these political authorities engage with treaties, i.e. whether the political authorities of a given subnational jurisdiction try to understand and deal with an international human rights treaty by working on and eventually taking, or trying to take, policy measures with a view to its (further) implementation.

At this stage, it is sufficient to say that when any actors use human rights treaties, their uses can lead to engagement by the relevant political authorities, but this is not always the case. To give an example, a local nongovernmental organisation (NGO) can use a treaty, e.g. by referring to an international treaty in a report, and this use can potentially result in an engagement of the cantonal legislator or other political authority, but it may also result in subnational authorities not engaging at all. We draw this distinction between use and engagement to clarify the sequence of pre-conditions taking place before the implementation and compliance stages.

Engaging with a treaty is not the same as implementing or complying with a treaty. When a state ratifies a human rights treaty, the state makes a commitment to 'perform the treaty in good faith' (art. 26 of the Vienna Convention on the Law of Treaties). When and how the subnational political authorities take note of the consequences of a treaty's obligations in their field of competence and make a commitment to (further) implementation is a process that requires further attention. Towards the end of this introduction, we will come back to the key notion of engagement, and we will explain why understanding the engagement of political authorities with a treaty is key to appreciate how human rights law works in practice in the subnational policy processes.

---

[1] 'Political authorities' is a widely used term including executive, legislative (and sometimes judicial) bodies—in our case, we do not include judicial bodies (Bauer et al., 2019).

Our research contributes to the 'international turn to the local' (Eslava, 2015) by examining the ways in which international human rights treaties shape aspects of 'everyday life for the people'. Indeed, we agree with Eslava that 'international law (…), is not a normative international—or supra-national—system secluded from national and local administrations and from the daily lives of people. On the contrary, the international attention that is currently being paid to local jurisdictions bears witness to the enmeshment of international law in national and local transformations, and in the material and subjective construction of the world' (Eslava, 2015, p. 293). It is the dynamic and iterative nature of subnational human rights uses and the political authorities' engagement with the treaties that we set out to explore.

In the following sections of this chapter, we will first justify the focus on subnational actors and their uses of human rights treaties (Sect. 1.2.1); second, we will explain why we concentrate on international human rights treaties containing obligations that require domestic policy measures (Sect. 1.2.2); third, we justify the focus on Switzerland (Sect. 1.2.3) and we then dedicate subsection 1.3 to explain what we mean by the political authorities' 'engagement with human rights treaties', which is a notion that provides more analytical leverage to understand what subnational authorities do with human rights treaties than a focus on implementation or compliance. We conclude this chapter with an overview of the organisation of the book.

1.2.1 Why Subnational Actors and Human Rights Treaties?

Subnational actors are key human rights actors. We concentrate on the trajectories of international treaties and on their consequences at the subnational level from an actor-centred perspective that also accounts for the context and the processes at work. Our motivation to focus on subnational actors is inspired by one of the most influential studies examining the effects of international human rights treaties at the domestic level: *Mobilizing Human Rights* by Beth Simmons (Simmons, 2012). Simmons argues that human rights treaties make a notable positive contribution to the concrete realisation of rights protection, particularly 'where they have domestic political and legal traction' (Simmons, 2012, p. 12). We read her book as an invitation to shed light on the intricacies of the 'least likely' processes: subnational actors are even more remote from foreign policy and international law-making than national actors upon whom studies on human rights law in domestic jurisdictions usually focus. The remoteness and high degree of separation of subnational actors provide them with considerable room for manoeuvre in implementation. Hence, a study into the uses subnational actors make of human rights treaties, the mechanisms through which subnational political authorities engage with international treaty obligations and how this engagement comes about is crucial to understand how contemporary international human rights law works in practice.

1.2.2 Why International Human Rights Treaties with Obligations Requiring the Adoption of Policy Measures?

Simmons writes about the power of treaties to constrain state behaviour (Simmons, 2012, p. 5), but not all human rights obligations are equal. Contemporary human rights law goes much beyond negative obligations (such as that states must abstain from torture) and includes a plethora of obligations requiring state actors to actively take measure to realise rights. We concentrate on treaties that contain obligations that require the adoption or change of policy measures because they are particularly demanding, and we seek to explain the variation in the engagement of subnational political authorities with them.

Contemporary international human rights norms regularly require the adoption of measures, and such measures must often include the adoption or change of existing domestic legal norms (Schmid, 2015). International human rights treaties, for instance, oblige states to have a legislative framework in place that effectively protects individuals from domestic violence. States must not only have legislation that criminalises domestic violence, but they must also have legislative provisions aiming to prevent domestic violence, to ensure that victims be fairly and respectfully treated by all actors and in all legal procedures, and legislators must allot budgets and allocate responsibilities, e.g. to provide for a sufficient number of shelter places. Such treaty obligations are called positive obligations because states cannot meet them by abstention but only by actively taking measures aiming at their implementation. They are often also legislative obligations because their implementation requires the contribution of lawmakers. Sometimes, international human rights treaties mention the compulsory adoption of legislative measures. More often, the legislator is not mentioned explicitly in the treaty itself but the contribution of the domestic legislators is necessary because the domestic competence lies with the legislative branch (Kaempfer, 2021; Schmid, 2015). We will now explain why we are particularly interested in treaty obligations requiring subnational political authorities to adopt new domestic norms, change existing ones or to adopt other concrete policy measures.

'Human rights treaties are difficult to implement' (Fraser, 2020, p. 111) and this is particularly so for positive obligations. Human rights treaties contain numerous obligations requiring the active contribution of domestic political authorities. As mentioned, these obligations cannot be complied with by mere abstention but require political choices about the concrete measures to be adopted and funded and this fact renders their implementation complex. As Robin West pointed out, there is a 'relative absence of questions about the positive duties of legislators, not negative duties to restrain from acting (such as a duty not to infringe upon speech) or negative duties to restrain from acting in particular ways (such as a duty not to legislate in discriminatory ways), but positive, affirmative duties to pass laws so as to achieve various (...) ends' (West, 2006, p. 221). This relative lack of research on positive international obligations is important because the predominant conception of statehood has changed over the past centuries towards a state that is expected to play a significant role in the prevention or mitigation of harm, the provision of services or the realisation of human rights, including in domains that used to be considered 'private spheres' (Clapham, 1996; Lavrysen, 2016). Our starting points are two treaties that contain numerous obligations requiring the active contribution of domestic political authorities. To examine how treaties containing such positive obligations unfold at the subnational level, we study the uses of two such treaties by subnational actors and how subnational political authorities, i.e. cantonal parliaments and governments, engage with these treaties.

The attention we pay to positive obligations at the subnational level and the uses of treaties by a variety of actors means that courts play a marginal role in this book. For a long time, international lawyers examining international law in domestic legal systems have tended to focus on tribunals, rather than on actors taking part in the political process (Ammann, 2020; Bjorge, 2015; McCrudden, 2015; Nollkaemper, 2011; Tzanakopoulos, 2011). We and the authors who studied international law in domestic courts share the underlying assumption that international jurisdiction and enforcement remain limited and national organs maintain a crucial role in shaping the reality of international law. Yet, a focus on domestic tribunals has major disadvantages: first, many challenges related to the implementation of international legal obligations are never addressed in the courtroom. It is a significant misconception to believe that human rights realisation happens primarily in courtrooms. Courts are important for human rights protection but most individuals whose everyday life is affected by human rights implementation gaps never litigate. Access to courts for insufficient implementation of human rights norms is far from obvious—for procedural, financial and sociological reasons (Arnardóttir, 2003). Moreover, when court cases arise, tribunals generally find themselves in a delicate position vis-à-vis the legislature because of separation of power issues, and a focus on tribunals only analyses situations in which there is (allegedly) already a 'pathology' in implementation. We, therefore, deliberately want to look elsewhere, namely on the actors who have the institutional competence and power to adopt the necessary policy measures and those who can use treaties to encourage the engagement of political authorities with human rights treaties.

In Switzerland, a focus on domestic courts falls particularly short. The Swiss Federal Supreme Court usually concludes that norms aimed (primarily) at a law-making organ are not directly applicable.[2] The approach of the Swiss

---

[2] Norms that are not directly applicable (or not self-executing) are norms that require legislative concretisation before a tribunal may use them to decide a case. A directly applicable norm is considered a legal provision that (a) is sufficiently concrete and precise in order to form the basis for a decision in a concrete case and (b) is addressed to the judicial organs and (c) describes rights and obligations of individuals, e.g. Decision of the Swiss Federal Supreme Court 136 I 297, c. 8.1. or 121 V 246. Whereas the concept of direct

Federal Supreme Court accentuates the fact that treaty obligations requiring legislative concretisation are usually not addressed in much detail by the Swiss courts, if at all. The relative lack of systematic analysis of subnational actors, rather than courts, and their uses of human rights treaties thus comes with serious drawbacks to our understanding of the complex relationships between international law and the domestic legal system. It is therefore of fundamental interest to study what subnational actors involved in subnational policy processes do with human rights treaties and to understand how they do it, when and through which mechanisms they do it and what explains the variations in the engagement of political authorities. As soon (or as long) as a constitutional system allocates competence at a subnational level, the subnational actors, first and foremost, the cantonal parliaments and the cantonal bureaucracies, will be the ones charged with the implementation of numerous treaty obligations and subnational actors inevitably become key players in furthering or denying rights implementation. Courts play second fiddle at best.

Despite the focus on domestic courts by international law scholars, legal scholars studying the complex interplay between international law and domestic legal systems have increasingly recognised the importance of domestic legislative actors for the effectiveness of international law (Beenakker, 2018; Cassese, 2012; MacNaughton & Duger, 2020; Slaughter & Burke-White, 2006). When the role of political actors, including legislators, has been examined, two main limitations remain: first, most studies have investigated the impact of a treaty on national legal systems and the domestic legislative outcomes (Keller & Stone Sweet, 2008; Risse et al., 2013; Simmons, 2012), but only very rarely the mechanisms and conditions behind the process leading to this effect (for a notable exception, see: Haglund & Stryker, 2015). Second, when the processes have been studied, the literature has so far mostly dealt with the legislative implementation of specific *judgements* of international tribunals, such as the European Court of Human Rights (Donald & Speck, 2020; Saul, 2021).

These studies offer fruitful insights into what others have called the 'drilling down in norm diffusion' (Restoy & Elbe, 2021) but they do not yet answer the question of how the actors use international human rights treaty norms in local processes and how these uses relate to the engagement of the relevant subnational political authorities in the absence of a previous court condemnation. We aim to understand how subnational political authorities engage with treaties in concrete cases, specifically in the most common scenarios in which no tribunal has sentenced the state for an implementation failure.

---

applicability is distinct from the concept of justiciability (i.e. the question of whether an issue can be decided by a judicial tribunal), the Swiss Federal Supreme Court traditionally (and problematically in our view) equates the lack of direct applicability with the lack of justiciability and vice-versa (Wyttenbach, 2017, p. 290f).

1.2.3 International Treaty Obligations at the Subnational Level in Switzerland

As mentioned, we collected our data in Switzerland. We focus on Switzerland because the implementation of human rights obligations is particularly complex in federal states and the role of subnational actors is especially relevant (Ku et al., 2019; Wyttenbach, 2017). Swiss subnational legislators, i.e. cantonal parliaments and the actors surrounding them offer a prime instance of understudied and yet crucial actors for the implementation of human rights treaties. In the chapter on subnational legislatures in the *Oxford Handbook of Legislative Studies* written by William Downs, the author ends by suggesting that increased attention to subnational legislatures is 'a pressing issue for the future' and will further our 'understanding of one of representative democracy's most overshadowed institutional layers' (Downs, 2014, p. 622). Downs complains that subnational legislatures have traditionally been viewed as being of nominal importance, despite the fact that they are 'intrinsically crucial to understanding governance and political behaviour' (Downs, 2014, p. 609). Indeed, Swiss cantons are anything but unimportant for human rights implementation.

Switzerland provides an ideal case for the study of how subnational actors use human rights treaties in policy processes. From a purely international legal point of view, the situation is simple: international law requires that the states fully implement all relevant human rights obligations and comply with international treaties no matter their internal organisation.[3] It is up to each state's own legal system to ensure that all levels of state authority do what is required by the state's international obligations. If a state fails to ensure implementation across its legal system, it incurs international state responsibility.[4] The Swiss Federal Constitution requires that all levels of the state shall respect international law (art. 5 al. 4). Those unfamiliar with the intricacies of human rights implementation might think that there is a smooth allocation of tasks and a pre-determined path to be taken when a state ratifies a new human rights treaty and incurs new obligations. In practice, however, subnational actors must first at least know about the existence of a relevant human rights treaty concerning them. As our data shows, this cannot be taken for granted. Subnational actors sometimes do not know that they have international obligations and what these obligations might mean. Once subnational actors know about a treaty,

---

[3] Art. 27 of the Vienna Convention on the Law of Treaties, 1155 UNTS 331, 23 May 1969 (entered into force 27 January 1980).

[4] Another state might complain about a lack of implementation in an interstate proceeding or by diplomatic means, but this option often remains theoretical. Or, depending on the specific issues at stake and what the state has consented to, an individual may be entitled to seek redress before a regional or an international body (such as the European Court of Human Rights), in which case the individual must first exhaust domestic remedies, also making this avenue a difficult endeavour—and the implementation of a potential judgment is then still not automatic.

such knowledge does of course not yet mean that the treaty and all its obligations will be implemented. The high number, diversity and autonomy of Swiss subnational units implies that there will inevitably be challenges with subnational human rights implementation. Moreover, Switzerland is a small country with an open economy that is not a member of the European Union. These features raise the relevance of an engagement with international law (Miaz et al., 2024). International treaties that require the adoption of policy measures thus create challenges for the Swiss legal system. We can group the reasons for these challenges into two groups.

The first specificity is that Swiss federalism is a highly decentred system organised in diverse units of a relatively small scale. The 26 subnational units are competent to legislate in relation to numerous international obligations and they enjoy large autonomy. Cantons have indeed 'considerable room for manoeuvre in significant political areas (e.g. education, culture, language, health care, law enforcement)' (Vatter, 2018, p. 104). Moreover, the Swiss legal system is considered monist, meaning that ratified international treaties become part of the Swiss legal system as soon as they enter into force. As soon as a human rights treaty binds Switzerland and contains at least one obligation that requires the adoption of policy measures that falls within a cantonal domain of competence and this treaty obligation is not already perfectly implemented in all cantons, up to 26 legislatures must become active and are supposed to engage with these obligations (Kaempfer, 2021). This means that the most important place where human rights realisation is shaped is regularly neither a courtroom nor a federal chamber, but the 26 cantons and their policy processes.

Second, Swiss subnational parliaments remain semi-professional, i.e. they are composed of members from various backgrounds who meet on a non-permanent basis (Pilotti, 2017). The identification of the various obligations in an international human rights treaty, the interpretation of treaty norms and the assessment of what measures seem necessary or suitable to implement them regularly require special expertise that is not, or at least not always, easily available to semi-professional parliaments or their secretariats. It is not surprising that this situation can at times overwhelm.

The Swiss division of competences comes with some opportunities but also with obvious complexity (Wyttenbach, 2017, pp. 559–560). The opportunities include the ability of cantons to consider the specificity of each context, increased legitimacy and ownership and the fact that dealing with multiple normative levels is a familiar task in the Swiss legal system. Moreover, new ideas can be tested in one canton and if they are successful, the ideas can later provide inspiration for another canton. At the same time, these structural aspects of the Swiss legal system suggest that it can be difficult for subnational authorities to engage with international treaties even in situations in which political will and leadership would be forthcoming. Wyttenbach summarises how the decentred situation may create delays in subnational implementation and favour the emergence of a reactive attitude whereby the federal level is expected to take the lead on the implementation of an international legal obligation. To this author, if federal engagement is not forthcoming, the likelihood of gaps between law in books and law in action at the subnational level increases (Wyttenbach, 2017, pp. 99–102).[5] These challenges and the crucial role of the cantons in the implementation of international human rights treaties strengthen the pertinence of undertaking research on the relation between international obligations, mechanisms and processes. Given the complexities of conducting empirical research in relation to international norms at the subnational level, it may be unsurprising that this gap in the field has not been filled. Generalisation is necessarily limited but our findings allow a number of important conclusions to be drawn about the socio-political uses of international human rights law in subnational law-making, and more broadly, in subnational policy processes, to understand how subnational actors relate to human rights obligations and are affected by them. Many of the processes of using human rights treaties are also available to actors in more centralised jurisdictions, including those who use treaties with the aim of furthering the engagement of a national assembly. We will return to the generalisation and needs for further research in Chapter 6.

We will now explain what we mean by the key notion of *engagement* with human rights treaties.

1.3 Key Terms: Subnational Political Authorities' Engagement with Human Rights Treaties

We employ the concept of *engagement* to convey the idea that political authorities (i.e. parliament and government) of a given subnational jurisdiction try to understand and deal with an international human rights treaty by working on and eventually taking, or trying to take, policy measures with a view to its (further) implementation. Engagement thus happens when actors holding institutional positions of power and influence *intend* to take steps towards implementing a treaty or parts thereof.

Readers may ask what the distinction is between *using* a treaty and *engaging* with a treaty. Engagement can be triggered by uses of the treaty but the two are distinct. We reserve the term engagement for the conduct of political authorities, and we only refer to 'engagement' when political authorities move towards the production of implementation outputs, i.e. when political authorities start proposing legislative reforms, action plans, or when they approve budgets, i.e. to grant (additional) financial or human resources. The outcome of an engagement can be legislative or other policy measures taken by subnational political authorities. The implementation of treaty obligations may not

---

[5] The author refers to 'silent negative conflicts of competence', i.e. the idea that neither the federal nor the cantonal actors feel responsible. Human rights supervisory mechanisms have criticised, inter alia, the relative lack of monitoring, compliance and follow-up structures at subnational level in federal states.

necessarily be successful, or it may be incomplete, and it may only in part be due to the existence of the international treaty. We consider that political authorities can engage with a treaty for a variety of reasons and the intention to improve implementation may not necessarily be the main motivation. Political authorities can, for instance, be interested in a legislative process to adopt a law on integrative schooling of children with disabilities and we do not attempt to argue that their main motivation is the implementation of the UN Convention on the Rights of Persons with Disabilities. Rather, we are interested in the process leading to the moment in which we can identify what we call engagement: the political authorities using the treaty to deal with the obligations and their implementation within their political sphere. The concept of engagement is significant because it denotes the key shift at which political authorities take up a treaty or some obligations of it and make some sort of implementation commitment. This crucial step has so far been overlooked in research and is sometimes even assumed as self-evident, but empirical reality shows that it is not. Engagement is only a pre-condition for implementation, and not a sufficient one, but a very crucial one. As we show in Chapter 5, such engagement may and often does stem from the uses that other actors make of the treaty, although by far not all uses lead to engagement. One of the main contributions of our analysis is precisely to shed light on the processes that lead up to an engagement by political authorities.

Engaging with a treaty may involve the legislative implementation of the obligations arising from the treaty, and result in the concrete implementation of these obligations. Engaging with a treaty can also mean creating an institution or a position to implement or prepare the implementation of the treaty, to grant additional (financial) resources to the responsible bureaucracy, to progressively change the policy paradigm according to the treaty. We do not establish causal links between uses, engagement and implementation. Rather, we show the complex and iterative process between various actors' uses of the treaties and the decision of political authorities to engage with a treaty and although we do not present causal data, we believe it is entirely reasonable to assume that such engagement is often useful to further concrete implementation. Political authorities engaging with a human rights treaty will usually mean that the political space for implementation tends to open or widen because political authorities show commitment to the treaty or at least some parts thereof.

But how do we know if political authorities act with a view towards implementation? Our definition of engagement presupposes that political authorities intend to implement at least to some extent a treaty or some of its obligations. If authorities simply refer to a treaty to dismiss its relevance, we will qualify the example as a use of the treaty, but not as an engagement. In doing so, we decided our analysis of engagement would include situations in which political authorities use a treaty as a cognitive resource (e.g. to convince members of a parliament to accept some measures) or mention a treaty as a legal basis for a legislative proposal that may also have been proposed for reasons other than the treaty. We acknowledge that political authorities may sometimes merely refer to a treaty as an add-on to an already decided course of action. Nevertheless, even in this scenario, the treaty gains in profile within the subnational jurisdiction and even a lukewarm commitment to further implementation is sometimes an entry-point for later and more significant engagements.

Other authors used the term 'engagement' differently. Krommendijk refers to 'engagement with a treaty' to capture both what he calls 'the impact and effectiveness' of a treaty obligation.[6] Unlike Krommendijk, we employ the notion of engagement independent of the effectiveness of a treaty obligation because we are interested in the genesis of the engagement as such, rather than the measurement of its effectiveness. Krommendijk speaks of the impact of the treaty whenever actors involved in legislative or policymaking processes have used or referred to the treaty or the obligation (Krommendijk, 2018, p. 231). In our study, referring to a treaty obligation is a use of a treaty and an engagement if the invocation of the treaty comes from political authorities who intend to move towards implementation.

Now that we have introduced the key notion of engagement, we move to explain why studying the uses of treaties by subnational actors and the engagement of subnational political authorities with treaties provides more analytical leverage than a focus on compliance or implementation would.

1.4 Why Focus on Engagement, Rather than Compliance or Implementation?

Let us begin by distinguishing compliance from implementation. Compliance exists 'when the actual behaviour of a given subject conforms to prescribed behaviour' (Raustiala & Slaughter, 2002). For international human rights law in federal states, compliance means that the conduct of subnational entities, in law and in fact, corresponds to what international obligations in the field of competence of the subnational units require. Considerable international research has been undertaken on compliance with international human rights (e.g. Cole, 2015; Hafner-Burton & Tsutsui, 2007; Hillebrecht, 2014).

Implementation is a process by which the obligations contained in the human rights treaties are translated into domestic law (legislative implementation) and are de facto realised so that human rights are protected in concrete individual situations (concrete implementation, usually taking place at the 'street level', e.g. by police officers or social workers). Legislative implementation does not necessarily result in concrete implementation, and concrete implementation may sometimes occur without previous legislative implementation. When a state succeeds in implementing all aspects of an international

---

[6] Krommendijk uses the term 'effectiveness' to describe the extent to which a treaty, a norm or an obligation has 'led to policy, legislation or any other measure' (while compliance merely requires a conformity of a treaty obligation and the policies and laws that are in place, even when no changes are needed to arrive at this conformity) (Krommendijk, 2018, p. 231).

obligation, that state is in full compliance. Some key studies on implementation include those by Keller & Stone Sweet (2008) and by Risse Ropp and Sikkink (1999, 2013), and those studies that focused on the implementation of international courts' judgements and decisions of human rights bodies (Beenakker, 2018; Betts & Orchard, 2014; Donald & Speck, 2020; Murray & Long, 2022). Simmons highlighted that, once ratified, treaties are likely to impact policymaking and 'alter politics' by setting goals for public policy and practice, by empowering domestic actors (see also Dai, 1999) with resources (knowledge, tools) and opportunities to claim for treaty implementation, and by setting the political agenda (Simmons, 2012). Previous implementation literature has thus shown that international human rights law can lead to domestic change resulting from domestic mechanisms and processes—to Simmons, agenda-setting, litigation, and political mobilisations (Simmons, 2012)—, or through a process of socialisation, whereby pressure on governments comes both 'from above' and 'from below' (Risse et al., 1999, p. 276).

The literatures on compliance and implementation relate to our study. We all aim to shed light on the conditions and factors influencing human rights realisation by domestic actors with human rights treaties, but—put simply— our attention on the *engagement* with treaties focuses on an earlier moment in the process in which domestic actors deal with human rights treaties. The focus on engagement has significant advantages.

First, focusing on engagement allows us to explain the key phenomena occurring in between the unawareness of treaties and full compliance. As Başak Çalı has convincingly argued, compliance with international law is often difficult to measure and a matter of degree rather than 'an either/or concept' (Çalı, 2015, p. 179). This underlines the importance of understanding what comes first: when the wheels are set in motion to commit to (further) implementation or compliance. In contrast to compliance studies, we do not aim to assess whether or to what extent subnational entities comply with international treaties or not, nor if they violate human rights. We place the focus on the uses of, and on political authorities' engagement with international treaties, rather than an evaluation of whether specific conduct falls within the categories of compliance *vs* non-compliance, obedience *vs* disobedience. We are not primarily interested in the final implementation outcomes nor the establishment of causal relationships between the use of treaties and the implementation of the obligations. Rather, we aim to understand the processes leading up to the engagement of the subnational political authorities with the treaties in the first place and how we can categorise and understand this engagement. We are interested in finding out how the engagement by subnational political authorities comes about because such an engagement is usually a key preliminary condition for later implementation or compliance. Our contribution is to explain the origins and patterns of the subnational political authorities' engagement with international treaties and the uses and factors encouraging such engagement.

Engagement with the treaty is often what leads to improved implementation and potentially compliance. A focus on compliance would provide information about the comparison between obligations and the situation in the examined state and at best the correlation between the outcome and various possible reasons. What we are most interested in, however, is not the examination of possible gaps between obligations and state conduct, but the uses of the treaties and the processes that can lead political authorities to engage with treaty obligations—paving the way for democratically legitimised subnational legislators to ensure the legislative implementation of the treaty,[7] and generally subnational political authorities' weight in policy processes improving rights realisation. As Howse and Teitel have remarked for Simmons' *Mobilizing for Human Rights*, 'going beyond rule compliance can produce illuminating quantitative and qualitative analysis of international law impacts' (Howse & Teitel, 2011, p. 813). We share this view. We believe that our focus on engagement allows us to shed light on the understudied but indispensable pre-conditions of compliance in many cases.[8]

Our approach (and specifically our focus on the uses of human rights treaties and on the notion of engagement) is inspired by Sally Merry's work. Like Sally Merry, we also use an actor-centred approach and, in Chapters 4 and 5 of the book, we take a bottom-up perspective to identify varieties of how subnational actors use human rights treaties and how subnational political authorities engage with treaties. Our empirical research is inspired by a shared motivation with her work to study how subnational or local actors use law. We notably borrow the concern for the 'translation' of norms to a local context (Merry, 2006). In her influential account, 'translation' does not necessarily favour 'justice' (or, to use the terms of our own study, an engagement with human rights that would favour the successful implementation). Rather, the notion of translation refers to the constitutive power of law and 'the meanings produced by law in the habitual, possibly resistant, practices of everyday life' (Merry, 1995, p. 25). Our research examines both this constitutive power of legal norms and the constructive understanding of norms contained within treaties.

That said, Sally Merry and those working with her have not been concerned about how the engagement with binding norms of international human rights law by political authorities comes about (let alone in a subnational entity). Sally Merry's main contribution lies in the social understandings and the local uses of legal norms but not the lead-up of political authorities' engagement with treaties. We take treaty obligations as starting points and therefore place more emphasis on legal bindingness than Sally Merry. But we do not assume that the

---

[7] Others similarly found a focus on compliance too narrow to understand how Europeanisation 'in action' plays out in member states in multi-level dynamics that occur simultaneously top-down and bottom-up (Schmidt, 2008; Thomann & Sager, 2017).

[8] The exception are cases in which a treaty is implemented without the treaty having played a role, e.g. because the status quo prior to ratification already perfectly complies with all obligations of a treaty—a scenario that is uncommon in practice.

legal bindingness of a norm necessarily determines implementation or even the engagement of domestic actors with international norms (to take into account a criticism of widespread assumptions in traditional legal scholarship already voiced by Karen Knop's work (Knop, 2000)). We are interested in examining the varieties in which subnational actors make use of legal bindingness, how they use the bindingness of a treaty in subnational policymaking processes, and what patterns of engagement by the political authorities we can identify. These processes are best captured by looking at the uses of treaties by subnational actors and the engagement by political authorities rather than the potential (but never automatic) implementation that can come after such engagement. We will expose the ways in which we pin down engagement in Chapter 2 where we present the empirical research design.

1.5   Organisation of the Book

Our book is structured into six chapters. This introduction explored the reasons for studying the role of subnational actors and the ways in which they use human rights treaties and when political authorities engage with treaties. The introduction is followed, in Chapter 2, by a detailed presentation of our approach, research design, methods and data on the uses of human rights at the subnational level and our justification for the selection of the case studies. We explain the ways in which we draw inspiration from methodological insights from previous studies to understand how uses of treaties can relate to the engagement of the subnational political authorities with the treaties. Our core analysis is divided into three chapters, Chapters 3, 4 and 5. Conclusions follow in Chapter 6.

In Chapter 3, we first explain how international human rights treaties are ratified in Switzerland's federalist, monist system and how this pre-ratification phase influences the later uses of the treaties and what mechanisms are later employed to stimulate the engagement of subnational political authorities. Chapter 3 is written from the point of view of actors who want or who are sometimes even legally required to facilitate the compliance of Switzerland with its treaty obligations and who often enjoy a privileged position within the Swiss multilevel system. These actors include individuals and offices at the level of the Confederation, inter-cantonal conferences, mandated experts, and sometimes civil society. These actors use available formal and informal domestic mechanisms to 'translate' international treaty obligations into concrete human rights measures at the subnational level, often with the ideal in mind that all cantons should engage with the treaty. They believe that treaty obligations must be implemented. Based on previous research, we use a classification of four categories of mechanisms aiming to orient, often from the top, the ways in which international law treaties can be implemented at a subnational level (namely, sanctions, rewards, awareness-raising and co-operation, see [Kaempfer, 2023]). For better or worse, one of us observed, in a previous study, that in the case of international human rights treaties in

Switzerland, almost exclusively one type of mechanisms is used: information/awareness-raising. What is more, we find that these mechanisms do not fall from the sky; they are themselves imbricated in a dynamic interaction with the uses of human rights treaties by subnational actors—which is the focus of Chapter 4. Thus, Chapter 3 cautions against simplistic assumptions that a domestic legal system disposes of a pre-arranged machinery to implement treaty obligations within its jurisdiction. Chapters 3 and 4 are complementary in that they analyse the same process from two interdependent perspectives.

In Chapter 4, we change perspective and focus on the subnational actors and their socio-political uses of human rights treaty obligations. We explore how subnational actors use human rights treaties or parts thereof in their fields of activity. Here, we focus on cantonal actors who are not necessarily interested in human rights treaties as such and who are not necessarily familiar with international law but may use a treaty or a specific obligation to advance their objectives. We observe that the various ways in which international human rights treaty obligations are used are part of everyday political realities 'on the ground': the use of treaties and their obligations is patchy, very variable, and sometimes leads to further, sometimes consequential, uses by the same or other actors, raising the awareness of the treaty and sometimes to nothing tangible, such as a failed trial balloon that lands somewhere and then fades into oblivion. The variety of uses of treaties or parts thereof shows that the processes are not a top-down and predictable phenomenon. Rather, the use of human rights treaties happens in a complex way. Where a use is perceived as successful, a use of a human rights treaty by one actor can lead to an iterative process of translating some of the treaty norms into strategies, day-to-day work and—as we will see in Chapter 5—sometimes the engagement by political authorities to, for instance, adopt a new law or put in place and finance new institutional structures. Chapter 4 also shows how the agendas of the subnational actors are in turn sometimes (re)framed by other subnational actors' understanding of a treaty and/or the framing of the social problem to be addressed.

Chapter 5 analytically categorises the patterns of engagement of political authorities with international treaties (or parts thereof) that require subnational units to take active measures. The typology identifies three distinct patterns of engagement. The first is *implementation-centred* engagement, which has the implementation of the treaty as its primary objective. The second is *initiating* engagement, which arises when no policy measures exist in the relevant policy domain. The third pattern is *embedded* engagement, which takes place as part of (or is embedded in) a more extensive project that goes beyond or runs parallel to the specific issue covered by the treaty and whose main goals are not the implementation of the treaty. The chapter also offers a comparative outlook to distil similarities and differences in the patterns of engagement of the Istanbul Convention and the Convention on the Rights of Persons with Disabilities. It does not come as a surprise that we find that context, notably the political balance of power and financial resources, matters. We also observe how the engagement by political authorities sometimes depends on the agency of committed and specialised individual actors using human rights treaties.

The sixth and final chapter reflects on the interpretation to be given to our finding that subnational actors remain crucial craftsmen and—women of human rights implementation. Our findings indicate that only a limited number of core subnational actors use international human rights treaties or parts thereof, but these uses can lead to further uses by other actors, and most significantly, to the engagement of political authorities. Specifically, we have observed how uses of human rights treaties can enable bottom-up dynamics that may ultimately shape subnational legislative implementation in significant ways. This finding implies that the strengthening and the support allocated to the engagement of subnational political authorities with human rights treaties is a decisive and worthwhile leverage for those who want to support human rights implementation in practice, so as to have a real impact on individuals' lives and their everyday possibilities to enjoy human rights protection.

We will emphasise the need for further research in this field and encourage interdisciplinary research on the empirical realities of international law outside courtrooms. Our research strategy can provide a blueprint for other researchers and practitioners who wish to study (or influence) the concrete engagement of subnational actors and ultimately the implementation of human rights obligations.

Finally, shedding light on the complex processes at the subnational level is of practical importance. As we explained in this introductory chapter, subnational actors are crucial to ensure that international human rights law is effective, but their remoteness and high degree of separation complexify implementation. Moreover, when implementation occurs successfully, the success stories are rarely at the forefront of public attention, and this lack of visibility can arguably lead to the inaccurate impression of a sweeping irrelevance of human rights law. At the time of writing, there is widespread scepticism towards international human rights treaties. It is time to critically review the ways in which human rights treaties are used at the subnational level, with real impact on people's everyday lives. While criticism of human rights is currently fashionable and some argue that human rights law needs some sort of 'saving' or 'fixing' (Moyn, 2018; Tasioulas, 2019; Wuerth, 2022), we caution that a focus on the day-to-day realities of human rights treaties in subnational policy processes is important. Human rights law is not a panacea for the problems of this world, but our results indicate that human rights norms have important but 'mundane' effects in domestic policy processes, away from the radar screen of mainstream legal literature (Van Ho et al., 2022). The engagement of subnational political authorities with international human rights treaties has real effects not only on subnational laws and policies but also on real people. A deeper understanding of the processes behind this engagement of subnational political authorities with human rights norms is an important safeguard against overly broad conclusions of the alleged inefficacity or—conversely—overreaching power of international human rights law.

As we will see throughout the book, subnational realities of whether or not a human rights treaty is known and used has real consequences. The subnational engagement of political authorities with international human rights treaties has in the past opened or widened the space for implementation progress. This can mean that the child next door with a disability can attend classes with their peers in the neighbourhood, a threatened woman knows where to find safety from domestic violence, the police officer questions her in a sensitive way or the person with an intellectual disability has regained the right to vote, to name just a few.

REFERENCES

Ammann, O. (2020). *Domestic Courts and the Interpretation of International Law: Methods and Reasoning Based on the Swiss Example*. Brill.

Arnardóttir, O. M. (2003). *Equality and Non-Discrimination under the European Convention on Human Rights*. Nijhoff.

Bauer, P., Freitag, M., & Sciarini, P. (2019). Political Trust in Switzerland: Again a Special Case. In J. Jedwab & J. Kincaid (Eds.), *Identities, Trust, and Cohesion in Federal Systems: Public Perspectives* (Vol. 197, pp. 115–146). Queen's Policy Studies. https://doi.org/10.2307/j.ctvdtpjdq.8

Beenakker, E. (2018). *The Implementation of International Law in the National Legal Order: A Legislative Perspective*. Leiden University.

Betts, A., & Orchard, P. (Eds.). (2014). *Implementation and World Politics: How International Norms Change Practice*. Oxford University Press.

Bjorge, E. (2015). *Domestic Application of the ECHR: Courts As Faithful Trustees*. Oxford University Press.

Çalı, B. (2015). *The Authority of International Law: Obedience, Respect, and Rebuttal*. Oxford University Press.

Cassese, A. (2012). Towards a Moderate Monism: Could International Rules Eventually Acquire the Force to Invalidate Inconsistent National Laws? In *Realizing Utopia: The Future of International Law* (pp. 187–199). Oxford University Press.

Clapham, A. (1996). *Human Rights in the Private Sphere*. Clarendon Press.

Cole, W. M. (2015). Mind the Gap: State Capacity and the Implementation of Human Rights Treaties. *International Organization, 69*(2), 405–441. https://doi.org/10.1017/S002081831400040X

Dai, X. (1999). The "Compliance Gap" and the Efficacy of International Human Rights Institutions. In T. Risse, S. C. Ropp, & K. Sikkink (Eds.), *The Power of Human Rights: International Norms and Domestic Change* (Vol. 66) (pp. 85–102). Cambridge University Press.

Donald, A., & Speck, A.-K. (2020). The Dynamics of Domestic Human Rights Implementation: Lessons from Qualitative Research in Europe. *Journal of Human Rights Practice, 12*(1), 48–70. https://doi.org/10.1093/jhuman/huaa007

Downs, W. (2014). Sub-National Legislatures. In S. Martin, T. Saalfield, & K. Strøm (Eds.), *The Oxford Handbook of Legislative Studies* (pp. 609–627). Oxford University Press.

Eslava, L. (2015). *Local Space, Global Life: The Everyday Operation of International Law and Development*. Cambridge University Press. https://doi.org/10.1017/CBO9781316135792

Fraser, J. (2020). *Social Institutions and International Human Rights Law Implementation: Every Organ of Society*. Cambridge University Press.

Gurowitz, A. (1999). Mobilizing International Norms: Domestic Actors, Immigrants, and the Japanese State. *World Politics, 51*(3), 413–445. https://doi.org/10.1017/S0043887100009138

Hafner-Burton, E., & Tsutsui, K. (2007). Justice Lost! The Failure of International Human Rights Law To Matter Where Needed Most. *Journal of Peace Research, 44*(4), 407–425.

Haglund, L., & Stryker, R. (2015). *Closing the Rights Gap: From Human Rights to Social Transformation*. University of California Press.

Hillebrecht, C. (2014). *Domestic Politics and International Human Rights Tribunals the Problem of Compliance*. Cambridge University Press.

Howse, R., & Teitel, R. (2011). Beth Simmons's Mobilizing for Human Rights: A Beyond Compliance Perspective Symposium: The 17th Annual Herbert Rubin and Justice Rose Luttan Rubin International Law Symposium: From Rights to Reality: Mobilizing for Human Rights and its Intersection with International Law. *New York University Journal of International Law and Politics, 44*, 813–818.

Kaempfer, C. (2021). Domestic Mechanisms for the Implementation of International Obligations in the Swiss Cantons. *Swiss Review of International and European Law, 31*(4), 541–563.

Kaempfer, C. (2023). *Les mécanismes de mise en oeuvre du droit international par les cantons suisses: études de cas dans les domaines des droits humains et des accords bilatéraux Suisse-UE*. Sui generis.

Keller, H., & Stone Sweet, A. (Eds.). (2008). *A Europe of Rights: The Impact of the ECHR on National Legal Systems*. Oxford University Press.

Knop, K. (2000). Here and There: International Law in Domestic Courts. *New York University Journal of International Law and Politics, 322*, 501–535.

Krommendijk, J. (2018). National Parliaments: Obstacles or Aid to the Impact of International Human Rights Bodies? In M. Wind (Ed.), *International Courts and Domestic Politics* (pp. 227–261). Cambridge University Press.

Ku, C., William, H., Stewart, D., & Diehl, P. (2019). Even Some International Law Is Local: Implementation of Treaties Through Subnational Mechanisms. *Virginia Journal of International Law, 60*(1), 105–158.

Lavrysen, L. (2016). *Human Rights in a Positive State: Rethinking the Relationship Between Positive and Negative Obligations Under the European Convention on Human Rights*. Intersentia.

MacNaughton, G., & Duger, A. (2020). Translating International Law into Domestic Law, Policy, and Practice. In *Foundations of Global Health & Human Rights* (pp. 113–131). Oxford University Press.

McCrudden, C. (2015). Why Do National Court Judges Refer to Human Rights Treaties? A Comparative International Law Analysis of CEDAW. *American Journal of International Law, 109*(3), 534–550.

Merry, S. E. (1995). Resistance and the Cultural Power of Law. *Law & Society Review, 29*(1), 11–26.

Merry, S. E. (2006). *Human Rights and Gender Violence: Translating International Law into Local Justice*. University of Chicago Press.

Miaz, J., Niederhauser, M., & Maggetti, M. (2024). From International Law to Subnational Practices: The Roles of Intermediaries in Translating the Istanbul Convention in Swiss Cantons. *Regulation & Governance, 18*(1), 121–138. https://doi.org/10.1111/rego.12523

Moyn, S. (2018). *Not Enough: Human Rights in an Unequal World*. Harvard University Press.

Murray, R., & Long, D. (Eds.). (2022). *Research Handbook on Implementation of Human Rights in Practice*. Edward Elgar Publishing.

Nollkaemper, A. (2011). *National Courts and the International Rule of Law*. Oxford University Press. http://public.ebookcentral.proquest.com/choice/publicfullrecord.aspx?p=1073493

Pilotti, A. (2017). *Entre démocratisation et professionnalisation: le Parlement suisse et ses membres de 1910 à 2016*. Seismo.

Raustiala, K., & Slaughter, A.-M. (2002). *Handbook of International Relations*. SAGE.

Restoy, E., & Elbe, S. (2021). Drilling Down in Norm Diffusion: Norm Domestication, "Glocal" Power, and Community-Based Organizations in Global Health. *Global Studies Quarterly, 1*(3), 1–10. https://doi.org/10.1093/isagsq/ksab025

Risse, T., Ropp, S. C., & Sikkink, K. (1999). *The Power of Human Rights: International Norms and Domestic Change* (Vol. 66). Cambridge University Press.

Risse, T., Ropp, S. C., & Sikkink, K. (2013). *The Persistent Power of Human Rights: From Commitment to Compliance*. Cambridge University Press.

Roosevelt, F. D. (1941). *President Franklin Roosevelt's Annual Message (Four Freedoms) to Congress*. Franklin D. Roosevelt Library.

Saul, M. (2021). Shaping Legislative Processes from Strasbourg. *European Journal of International Law, 32*(1), 281–308.

Schmid, E. (2015). The Identification and Role of International Legislative Duties in a Contested Area: Must Switzerland Legislate in Relation to «Business and Human Rights»? *Swiss Review International and European Law 25*(4), 563–589.

Schmidt, S. K. (2008). Beyond Compliance: The Europeanization of Member States through Negative Integration and Legal Uncertainty. *Journal of Comparative Policy Analysis: Research and Practice, 10*(3), 299–308. https://doi.org/10.1080/13876980802231016

Simmons, B. (2012). *Mobilizing for Human Rights: International Law in Domestic Politics*. Cambridge University Press.

Slaughter, A.-M., & Burke-White, W. (2006). The Future of International Law Is Domestic (or, The European Way of Law). *Harvard International Law Journal, 47*(2), 327–352. https://doi.org/10.1093/acprof:oso/9780199231942.001.0001

Tasioulas, J. (2019). Saving Human Rights From Human Rights Law. *Vanderbilt Journal of Transnational Law, 52*(5), 1167–1207.

Thomann, E., & Sager, F. (2017). Moving Beyond Legal Compliance: Innovative Approaches to EU Multilevel Implementation. *Journal of European Public Policy, 24*(9), 1253–1268. https://doi.org/10.1080/13501763.2017.1314541

Tzanakopoulos, A. (2011). Domestic Courts in International Law: The International Judicial Function of National Courts. *Loyola International and Comparative Law Review, 34*, 133–168.

Universal Declaration of Human Rights, GA res. 217A (III), A/810 at 71, 10 December 1948.

Van Ho, T., López, R., & Schmid, E. (2022, March 8). Deprioritizing Human Rights Will Not Protect Territorial Sovereignty. *Just Security*. https://www.lawfareblog.com/international-law-and-russian-invasion-ukraine

Vatter, A. (2018). *Swiss Federalism: The Transformation of a Federal Model*. Routledge.

West, R. (2006). Unenumerated Duties. *University of Pennsylvania Journal of Constitutional Law*, 9, 221–261.

Wuerth, I. (2022, February 25). International Law and the Russian Invasion of Ukraine. *Lawfare*. https://www.lawfareblog.com/international-law-and-russian-invasion-ukraine

Wyttenbach, J. (2017). *Umsetzung von Menschenrechtsübereinkommen in Bundesstaaten: gleichzeitig ein Beitrag zur grundrechtlichen Ordnung im Föderalismus*. Dike Verlag AG.

Open Access This chapter is licensed under the terms of the Creative Commons Attribution 4.0 International License (http://creativecommons.org/licenses/by/4.0/), which permits use, sharing, adaptation, distribution and reproduction in any medium or format, as long as you give appropriate credit to the original author(s) and the source, provide a link to the Creative Commons license and indicate if changes were made.

The images or other third party material in this chapter are included in the chapter's Creative Commons license, unless indicated otherwise in a credit line to the material. If material is not included in the chapter's Creative Commons license and your intended use is not permitted by statutory regulation or exceeds the permitted use, you will need to obtain permission directly from the copyright holder.

CHAPTER 2

Designing Research for Studying How Subnational Actors Use International Human Rights Treaties

Abstract This book examines how subnational actors use international human rights treaties and how subnational political authorities, including subnational legislators, come to engage with international treaties. In this chapter, we present our empirical approach, our research design, methods and data. We outline how we combine top-down and bottom-up perspectives, building on scholarship from law, political science and socio-legal studies. We explain and justify the selection of the treaties under investigation and the procedure of data collection for the Swiss case.

Keywords Convention on the Rights of Persons with Disabilities · Federalism · Interdisciplinarity · Intermediation · Istanbul Convention on Preventing and Combating Violence against Women and Domestic Violence · New Legal Realism

2.1 Restating the Research Objectives

The argument developed in this book begins with two international human rights treaties: the Istanbul Convention on Preventing and Combating Violence against Women and Domestic Violence (IC), and the UN Convention on the Rights of Persons with Disabilities (CRPD). Both of these treaties contain obligations requiring subnational political authorities to adopt measures, i.e. to engage actively with them by 'translating' an international obligation to a specific context so as to achieve the full realisation of the protected rights, such as the right to de facto equality by persons with disabilities (Schmid, 2015). In federal states, such as Switzerland, many of these obligations fall within the competences of subnational entities, which underlines the importance of subnational actors for human rights (see Chapter 1). Our overall concerns are first, to understand how subnational actors *use* international human rights treaties and second, how subnational political authorities, such as the cantonal parliament and the cantonal government, *engage* with international human rights treaties, i.e. work on and take policy and legislative measures to deal with an international treaty with a view to its (further) implementation. We invite readers to consult the introductory chapter for a detailed explanation of what we mean by *using* treaties and *engaging* with them. This chapter presents our approach, research strategy and design. We specifically explain important choices, our methods and the data collection.

International human rights law is expanding continuously. Today, human rights obligations percolate into many policy fields, requiring states to adopt policy measures to implement obligations arising from treaties (Schmid, 2015, p. 14). In federal states, to various degrees, the responsibility for the legislative implementation of human rights treaties lies not only at the central level but also at the subnational one (Ku et al., 2019; Schmid, 2019; Wyttenbach, 2018). What subnational entities do with human rights treaties—sometimes bypassing the nation-state—is thus key in understanding the domestic implementation, the effectiveness, and the realisation of human rights. Despite rich streams of research, subnational actors—above all, subnational legislators—are largely overlooked in studies on the implementation of international human rights law in domestic legal systems. To fill this gap, we focus on the mechanisms of engagement and on the socio-political uses of international human rights law in Swiss subnational policy processes, to understand how subnational actors use human rights treaties, and when and through what patterns the subnational authorities engage with the treaties.

This chapter presents our innovative approach and research strategy, which combines two complementary perspectives. On the one hand, we study the dynamics of processes related to the uses of international human rights treaties within domestic legal systems through *top-down processes*. On the other hand, following new legal realism, notably the stream of literature on legal intermediaries, we take a *bottom-up perspective* to study how actors involved in subnational legislative and policymaking processes use international treaties, understand them, make sense of them, interpret them, and contribute to the translation of obligations into concrete legislative reforms and policy measures more broadly.

In the following sections, we discuss the interdisciplinary nature of our approach, based on law studies, political science and socio-legal scholarship. As mentioned in Chapter 1, we put forward the notion of engagement to grasp what political authorities (parliaments, governments, administrations) do when they consider the relevance of international human rights treaties with a view to their (further) implementation. The various uses of the treaties by a wide range of subnational actors can sometimes lead to an engagement of the subnational political authorities with treaty obligations and ultimately to the adoption of concrete measures implementing the obligations. To justify our focus on the uses and engagement with treaties, we begin by discussing the various bodies of literature on which we build, and then we present how we selected the treaties that we studied and the procedure of data collection.

2.2 Identifying the Engagement of Subnational Actors with Human Rights Treaties: An Interdisciplinary Endeavour

A study into the processes by which human rights treaties are used and sometimes serve to orientate the engagement of subnational political authorities with treaties is necessarily interdisciplinary.

Such a research endeavour first requires legal analysis. In our study, we used doctrinal legal research to identify treaty obligations and to determine if a treaty contains obligations that fall within cantonal competences (Kaempfer, 2023; Schmid, 2015). The existence and interpretation of obligations requiring policy measures are sometimes contested in concrete cases. Hence, we assessed the legal arguments advanced in favour and against the existence of contested legal obligations in the treaties we include in our study. We employed legal reasoning based on the Vienna Convention of the Law of Treaties of 1969, domestic constitutional law and the domestic rules of legal interpretation.

Second, our research questions call for a political science perspective geared towards legislative activities (Milet, 2020), but also towards multilevel policy-making and regulatory governance (Maggetti, 2021; Maggetti & Trein, 2019; Thomann, 2015; Thomann & Sager, 2017; Thomann et al., 2019). This literature is useful to identify the sequences of the policy processes through which international human rights treaties are used by various types of political actors (e.g. agenda-setting and policy formulation). Political science literature also provides a methodological framework for devising our comparative case study strategy and selecting relevant subnational units to study, thus enabling us to observe when and how subnational actors use treaties and to explain variations in the patterns of engagement of subnational political authorities with international treaties.

Third and finally, socio-legal studies, especially the sociology of law, are of course indispensable for our purposes. Within socio-legal studies, we specifically built our approach on three streams of literature: domestic human rights legal implementation studies, New Legal Realism applied to international human rights law, and the emerging stream of literature on legal intermediation. This section discusses how these three streams of scholarship are useful to answer our research questions. We hope this outline of our approach can provide inspiration for complementary research in other contexts (see Chapter 6).

2.2.1 Studies on Domestic Human Rights Legal Implementation

First, we rely on research on the dynamics of domestic human rights legal implementation. As mentioned in Chapter 1, our book focuses on the engagement of political authorities with human rights treaties rather than implementation. That said, the literature on domestic human rights legal implementation is an important source of inspiration for our approach as we particularly build on insights from Beth Simmons' *Mobilizing for Human Rights*, as well as from studies by Jasper Krommendijk, and by Alice Donald and Anne-Katrin Speck. In terms of research design, for example, Krommendijk analysed public documents, conducted interviews, and performed database searches to determine the impact of recommendations of human rights committees on domestic parliaments in three states (Krommendijk, 2018). Our research design also combines the intensive research on public documents such as parliamentary debates and reports, as well as bureaucratic and civil society reports and communications, with semi-structured interviews to identify where, when, how and by whom treaties were understood, interpreted and used in cantonal policy processes. Moreover, we follow a methodological approach based on process-tracing (Beach & Pedersen, 2019; Bennett & Checkel, 2012; George & Bennett, 2005; Kapiszewski & Taylor, 2013). Donald and Speck applied process-tracing to the study of the implementation of international human rights judgments concerning structural violations in three European countries between 2016 and 2018 and found that the process is dynamic and iterative (Donald & Speck, 2020, pp. 50–51). They used a timeline to trace the impact of the judgments, showing that their influence varies a lot. We use the method of process-tracing as an inspiration: we also start from a top-down perspective that aims to trace the subnational implementation process of specific treaties (Chapter 3). In doing so, we contribute to deepen the understanding of how the engagement of political authorities 'may be constrained or enabled both by pre-existing conditions—structural, political and attitudinal—and by external developments that cause the political space for implementation to open or close' (Donald & Speck, 2020, p. 51).

2.2.2 New Legal Realism in Human Rights Scholarship

Second, we add to the research design from the domestic human rights implementation literature the insights gained from New Legal Realism literature and sociology of law related to human rights. Instead of limiting ourselves to the top-down perspective of the mentioned implementation studies, our approach combines the top-down perspective with a bottom-up one, geared towards grasping how subnational actors come to use international human rights treaties in measures adopted through subnational policymaking processes. This perspective is broader as it pays significant attention to subnational actors' points of view and activities to make sense of international human rights treaty law. It is rooted in a New Legal Realist approach of international law (Garth, 2006; Haglund & Stryker, 2015; Holtermann & Madsen, 2021; Klug & Merry, 2016; Merry, 2006b; Shaffer, 2016). New Legal Realism 'emphasizes the social context of law and seeks to develop approaches that account for how law actually works in action' (Talesh et al., 2021). Thus, we ask 'how actors use and apply law in order to advance our understanding of (…) how law obtains meaning, is practiced (the law-in-action), and changes over time' (Shaffer, 2015, p. 189). Haglund and Stryker (2015) have highlighted the wide variety of mechanisms and actors involved in the concrete pathways of rights realisation, and how these pathways are multilevel institutional processes. In line with these authors, we also focus on mechanisms, actors, and processes through which subnational authorities engage with human rights treaties.

Several scholars specifically analysed implementation processes of human rights of persons with disabilities. Pierre-Yves Baudot underlines that it makes sense to expand the focus beyond delays and implementation gaps because 'an analysis of implementation processes shows (…) that the diffusion of these [human rights] norms can take much more complex forms than a simple opposition between adaptation and resistance' (Baudot, 2018, p. 128). Baudot argues that 'the transfer [of new international norms is] not characterized by a thorough rethinking of the public policy subsystem, but [can] rather result […] in layering new rights on top of old frameworks' (Baudot, 2018, p. 117). Based on interviews with workers with disabilities in Belgium and with persons with either visual or mobility impairments in France, Lejeune and Ringelheim (2019) and Revillard (2018, 2019, 2023) studied rights consciousness, legal mobilisation, and rights realisation. While these studies take the CRPD into account, they understandably do not focus on the authorities' engagement. They underline the role of social movements, bureaucracies, and persons with disabilities in rights enforcement and enhancement (Lejeune & Ringelheim, 2019; Revillard, 2018, 2019), while noting major implementation problems (Revillard, 2023). These insights are important to us, as they invite us to consider the complex policy processes in which international human rights treaties are used by a variety of actors, including political authorities (parliaments, governments, bureaucracies), but also civil society organisations, social movements, and people most directly concerned by these rights.

As previously mentioned in Chapter 1, the seminal work of Sally Merry is indispensable to us as she asks how human rights become effective in local settings, by focusing on how they are 'translated into local terms and situated within local contexts of power and meaning' (Merry, 2006a, p. 1). In doing so, Merry shows how human rights become 'vernacular' (Levitt & Merry, 2009; Merry, 2006a), meaning that 'ideas and practices from the universal sphere of international organizations' become extracted and translated 'into ideas and practices that resonate with the values and ways of doing things in local contexts' (Merry & Levitt, 2017, p. 213). This New Legal Realist perspective on human rights and vernacularisation motivated us to systematically explore in two case studies the ways international human rights treaties are used, adapted and translated to fit diverse Swiss subnational contexts, taking into account the unique characteristics and political struggles of each subnational unit. As we will demonstrate, the two studied treaties require an adaptation to local context to eradicate or at least attenuate a structural human rights problem in a complex multilevel system, i.e. violence against women and the rights of persons with disabilities. By far and large, simple legislative incorporation does not suffice: what states, including their subnational entities, need to do is to engage with treaty obligations to make political decisions about the concrete measures to be implemented.

2.2.3 Intermediaries

The third body of literature we use is the literature on intermediaries. Sally Merry is of crucial importance again as she highlights the role of 'intermediaries such as community leaders, nongovernmental organization participants, and social movements activists [who] play a critical role in translating ideas from the global arena down and from local arenas up' (Merry, 2006c, p. 38).[1] To Sally Merry, intermediaries shape the practice of human rights by 'translat[ing] between human rights concepts and specific situations' and by 'translat[ing] international documents into terms relevant to particular localized political struggles' (Merry, 2006b, p. 978). The concept of intermediaries is also adopted by political scientists to highlight the function performed by actors mediating by rule-makers and rule-takers: they speak about regulatory intermediaries (Abbott et al., 2017; Miaz et al., 2024; Pegram, 2017). In the field of law and society, the notion of legal intermediaries and legal intermediation focus on how actors handle legal rules, and how the content and meaning of the rules are constructed in local settings: 'legal intermediaries play an increasing role in not just affecting, controlling or monitoring relations between rule-makers and rule-takers but also constructing the content and meaning of law itself' (Talesh & Pélisse, 2019, p. 138). These authors advocate for a bottom-up, interactive and inclusive approach taking into account the varieties of legal intermediaries, be they legal or non-legal actors, occupying a formal or informal function (Gray & Pélisse, 2019; Pélisse, 2019). Accordingly, 'rule intermediaries [are] state, business, and civil society actors that affect, control or monitor how legal rules are interpreted, implemented or constructed once they are passed by public legal institutions, facilitate, and inhibit social change in society' (Talesh & Pélisse, 2019, p. 113). This

---

[1] Shaffer also underlines the role of intermediaries in transnational legal processes. 'Operat[ing] at the national or subnational level' and 'offering multiple 'ports of entry' for transnational legal norms', these intermediaries 'help to diagnose national situations, monitor national developments and responses, and translate, adapt, and appropriate global norms for local contexts' (Shaffer, 2012, p. 254).

literature shows that varieties of intermediaries are involved in legal intermediation processes, including many actors who are not legal professionals (Pélisse, 2019) and who can be situated at different 'levels', not only 'macro-level actors' (e.g. actors of a 'reform network' at the national level) but also micro-level ones (e.g. managers and directors of bureaucracies) (Vincent, 2019), and 'insider activists' within organisations (Butcher, 2019).

These authors' understanding of intermediaries is a central feature of our own approach, as this approach allows us to operationalise the role of specific actors (intermediaries) in the Swiss federal system and the ways these intermediaries contribute to translate international human rights treaties into the subnational context. By analysing the contingent and processual aspects of legal intermediation (Billows et al., 2019) between a treaty, subnational authorities' engagement and, eventually, its implementation at different levels of the state, we can highlight 'not only the process by which rule-makers influence rule-takers', but also the 'tools, instruments, and hybrid categories used by these intermediaries and their participation in law in action, sometimes law in the books and often ordinary legality as defined by legal consciousness studies' (Pélisse, 2019, p. 106). Merry's and Pélisse's works notably inspired us to draft interview questions that allow us to understand the processes through which international law is translated into concrete subnational policy measures, and this literature was also useful in informing our selection of interview partners.

In summary, a combination of law, political science and socio-legal scholarship provide the ingredients for our own approach aiming to understand how subnational actors use human rights treaties and how subnational political authorities engage with the treaties. Next, we explain our choice to focus on the two selected human rights treaties.

2.3 Selecting the International Treaties

To answer our research questions in light of the theoretical discussion presented above, we chose two international treaties ratified by Switzerland which contain numerous obligations falling within subnational competences: the Council of Europe Convention on Preventing and Combating Violence against Women and Domestic Violence, known as the Istanbul Convention (IC, ratified by Switzerland in 2017), and the United Nations Convention on the Rights of Persons with Disabilities (CRPD, ratified by Switzerland in 2014). The two studied treaties cover different subject matters and contain different obligations; however, they do share some common ground which were the reasons why we selected them for this study. We selected these two treaties for two main reasons: first, they both contain numerous and relatively specific obligations that require ambitious policy measures at the Swiss subnational level, they are often relatively precisely worded and fall within the competences of the Swiss cantons (i.e. the subnational entities) and second, Switzerland ratified them relatively recently.

Treaties with ambitious and specific obligations are particularly suitable for our research. Specific obligations alleviate interpretative uncertainties and leave subnational actors with certain room for manoeuvre in using treaty obligations, engaging with them and, more generally, in linking the content of a treaty with their work or a public problem. Moreover, these treaties contain obligations, definitions and approaches that can be interpreted and adapted to local contexts, and eventually implemented through a variety of possible policy measures. In addition, subnational actors have certain room for manoeuvre to engage with these obligations and to use the content of a treaty (definitions, policy approach and paradigm). Recent treaties come with increased public attention (ratification message and parliamentary debate at the federal level, media attention, etc., see Chapter 3) and we can therefore expect subnational actors to take notice of the treaty, or at least that actors directly concerned by the treaty (politicians committed to the field concerned by the treaty, specialised policy bureaucrats, frontline workers, civil society organisations, social movements and people concerned) know that the treaty exists. Moreover, the recent ratifications of these two treaties facilitate the identification of relevant actors for the qualitative interviews we conducted because the subnational policy processes for implementation are recent or ongoing.

We now explain how the two selection criteria—obligations requiring ambitious policy measures at the subnational level and recent ratification—are met by the two selected treaties.

2.3.1 The Istanbul Convention

The Convention on Preventing and Combating Violence against Women and Domestic Violence, known as the Istanbul Convention (IC) was adopted by the Committee of Ministers of the Council of Europe on 7 April 2011 and was signed by Switzerland on 11 September 2013, ratified on 14 December 2017, and it entered into force for Switzerland on 1 April 2018.

The Istanbul Convention (IC) contains numerous obligations in the cantonal sphere of competences and many of these obligations are ambitious and relatively precisely worded. Presented as 'very significant' (McQuigg, 2012, p. 959), 'the most advanced' (De Vido, 2017, p. 69), 'potentially powerful' (Grans, 2018, p. 136) international human rights treaty targeting the elimination of violence against women and domestic violence, the IC brings a holistic approach to combating violence against women, requiring legislative and other policy measures in different fields, including civil and criminal law, law enforcement, social policies and awareness-raising to eradicate gender stereotypes. It takes a comprehensive gender and human rights perspective on violence against women and domestic violence and firmly establishes a link between achieving gender equality and the eradication of violence against women.² The IC frames violence against women as a structural problem. The structural nature of violence is considered in the preamble as 'one of the crucial social mechanisms by which women are forced into a subordinate position compared with men'.³ This means that states are obliged to eradicate a structural problem and it is only logical that this requires measures going beyond mere incorporation or abstention. To eradicate this violence, the obligations of the IC centre around four pillars (prevention, protection of victims, prosecution and co-ordinated policies), all of which fall almost exclusively within the cantonal competences in Switzerland.⁴ Compared to older human rights treaties focusing on equality, such as the UN Convention on the Elimination of Racial Discrimination (UNCERD), or even the UN Convention on the Elimination of all Forms of Discrimination against Women (CEDAW), the Istanbul Convention is longer (more than twice as long in terms of the number of words) and contains more detailed obligations to change domestic legislation and public policies. Such obligations can be general: 'parties shall take the necessary legislative and other measures to promote and protect the right for everyone, particularly women, to live free from violence in both the public and the private sphere' (art. 4 IC); or related to the approach and framing of the public problem: state parties 'shall undertake to include a gender perspective in the implementation and evaluation of the impact of the provisions of this Convention and to promote and effectively implement policies of equality between women and men and the empowerment of women' (art. 6 IC). The general obligations are complemented with numerous specific obligations, all of which require the allocation of resources, thus budgets, and therefore the participation of subnational political authorities. States are explicitly required to train professionals, students, pupils, the media and the private sector to challenge gender stereotypes, to protect victims from further violence through a range of specific preventive measures, to have ambitious legislation on police investigations, the prosecution of perpetrators and witness protection, and to monitor and potentially revise their legislation for gender-sensitive policies.⁵ Given that one of the purposes of the IC is to 'design a comprehensive framework, policies and measures for the protection of and assistance to all victims of violence against women and domestic violence' (art. 1 IC), it is not surprising that several articles relate to specific

---

² Council of Europe, 'Convention on Preventing and Combating Violence against Women and Domestic Violence,' Istanbul, 11 May 2011, Preamble; Council of Europe, 'Explanatory Report to the Council of Europe Convention on Preventing and Combating Violence against Women and Domestic Violence,' Istanbul, 11 May 2011, p. 5, §25.

³ Istanbul Convention, Preamble.

⁴ With the exception of federal criminal law, but the implementation of policing is a cantonal matter.

⁵ Based on Council of Europe, 'The Four Pillars of the Istanbul Convention', Brochure, https://rm.coe.int/coe-istanbulconvention-brochure-en-r03-v01/1680a06d4f (last consultation on 24 October 2023).

policy instruments, such as the obligations to provide shelters or to set up telephone helplines for victims:

> Parties shall take the necessary legislative or other measures to provide for the setting-up of appropriate, easily accessible shelters in sufficient numbers to provide safe accommodation for and to reach out pro-actively to victims, especially women and their children. (art. 23 IC)

> Parties shall take the necessary legislative or other measures to set up state-wide round-the-clock (24/7) telephone helplines free of charge to provide advice to callers, confidentially or with due regard for their anonymity, in relation to all forms of violence covered by the scope of this Convention. (art. 24 IC)

A detailed explanatory report, prepared by the Council of Europe, complements the normative landscape and provides additional information about the interpretation of the obligations of the Istanbul Convention, as well as sometimes very specific recommendations about the implementation based on the Council of Europe's previous work to combat violence against women (such as a specific, numbered, recommendation on the number of specialised women's shelter places in relation to the population size: 'one family place per 10,000 head of population').[6] In short, the Istanbul Convention is an international treaty with numerous and precise obligations, which are further detailed with a dense explanatory report, which makes the treaty more accessible to a range of actors. Taking all of this into account makes the Istanbul Convention a suitable case study for our purposes.

2.3.2 *The UN Convention on the Rights of Persons with Disabilities*

Our second case study revolves around the United Nations Convention on the Rights of Persons with Disabilities (CRPD). As the Istanbul Convention, the CRPD is part of the human rights treaties Switzerland ratified relatively recently. The CRPD was adopted on 13 December 2006, ratified by Switzerland on 15 April 2014 and entered into force for Switzerland on 15 May 2014.

The CRPD is also a human rights treaty containing ambitious and relatively precisely worded obligations and many of the obligations fall within the cantonal competences, such as those concerning education, employment, health and social protection services. The CRPD also addresses structural human rights inequality, this time especially in relation to persons with disabilities.[7] The CRPD requires, just like the Istanbul Convention, a progressive

---

[6] Council of Europe, 'Explanatory Report to the Council of Europe Convention on Preventing and Combating Violence against Women and Domestic Violence,' para. 135.

[7] The two can of course and unfortunately often do intersect given that women and girls with disabilities are particularly vulnerable to violence as a recent meta-study clearly indicates: (Sasseville et al., 2022).

framing of a public problem: the social conception of disability, as opposed to a medical one. Persons with disabilities shall have the same rights and opportunities as those without disabilities and to achieve this, physical and social obstacles must be removed, rather than placing the focus on how persons with a disability can adapt to the society around them. The CRPD thus stresses the autonomy and equality of persons with disabilities and invites us to place the emphasis on the way society is organised, rather than the individual's impairment. To achieve the aims of the CRPD, states must adopt or update legislation and policies in the following fields: they must ensure that persons with disabilities enjoy legal capacity on an equal basis with others in all aspects of life; to ensure de facto accessibility of infrastructure, transportation, communication services, culture and all other facilities or services open or provided to the public, on an equal basis with others. Most importantly, states must ensure their legislation and policies promote the inclusion in society of persons with disabilities, i.e. their right to live independently and participate fully in all aspects of life. In a federal state like Switzerland, the CRPD thus places ambitious and numerous demands upon the cantons. As with the Istanbul Convention, the obligations are numerous, and relatively precise and many of them fall squarely within the fields of competence of subnational units and require the adoption of wide-ranging measures suitable for the specific context of each canton and supported with the necessary allocation of resources. 'Simply' incorporating these obligations into national law, i.e. making national or subnational law contain the same obligations, is clearly insufficient here too.

The CRPD participates in a global 'paradigm shift' on disability, from a 'welfare model' to a 'civil rights model' (Quinn & Flynn, 2012), i.e. from a 'century of thinking about disability as an issue of welfare', in connection with a 'medical model' understanding disability as a result of individual impairments, towards a 'thinking about disability as an issue of equal rights, inclusion, dignity, and, most crucially, human rights', in connection with a 'social model' focusing on 'disabling environments and attitudes' as the sources of disability (Heyer, 2015, p. 2). Hence, this 'social model' understands disability as a social product, i.e. as a result of social and environmental barriers (Oliver, 2009). In sum, this treaty reaffirms that all persons with disabilities must enjoy all human rights and fundamental freedoms.

2.3.3   Reflections on This Treaty Selection

Does a selection of two treaties suffice to respond to our research questions? Two concerns must be addressed. First, one could argue that the recent nature of the two treaties skews our data as recent treaties may be easier to use and the engagement of subnational political authorities more forthcoming than for treaties that have been around for a long time. While we cannot rule out the possibility of this effect, we believe that even if it were present, it would not undermine the potential of our findings to be relevant beyond the selected two treaties. The benefit of focusing on two recent treaties is clearly a pragmatic one: the dynamics we are interested in studying are more easily observable. At the same time, such complex and demanding treaties also offer a hard case scenario, for which the same dynamics are expected to hold in less demanding cases. If we understand how these treaties are used, despite the implementation challenges they pose and the potential for resistance, the same dynamics can be expected to play out in at least similar ways with other treaties. Given that the range of required measures for both treaties involve significant financial resources, one could expect the financial implications to limit the engagement. Therefore, both treaties contain obligations that can be seen as hard cases.

Second, could one argue that issues related to the protection from violence and to persons with disabilities are at least somewhat more consensual than, for instance, issues explicitly related to racial discrimination or traveller communities, and that our data might therefore present the engagement of political authorities more forthcoming than what one might find when studying different treaties? We do not believe that the social perceptions of those protected by the treaties selected for our case studies create some bias in the data. We are confident to conclude that both treaties refer to numerous aspects that are not dealt with only thanks to an unequivocally high level of popular support. Suffice it to say that the idea of independent choices of how, where and with whom people with 'severe' disabilities live requires radical change compared to what is now common in Swiss cantons, where the landscape remains heavily institutionalised. Furthermore, as mentioned, the Istanbul Convention requires much more than police interventions—eradicating gender stereotypes is certainly not an uncontroversial matter these days. Last but not least, intersectionality is a reality and complexifies the superficial and in our view erroneous impression that issues related to protection from violence might be more consensual than other human rights issues. We can consider Switzerland's recently renewed reservation to Article 59 of the Istanbul Convention as a strong indication of this point: Article 59 obliges states to increase the protection of migrant women when their residence status increases their vulnerability.[8] It can thus certainly not be concluded that our observations are limited to a sub-set of rather consensual treaty obligations for which we observe numerous uses and engagement. Instead, the focus on two recent treaties with complex obligations offers meaningful insights for the study of human rights treaties at the subnational level.

In addition to the selection of the two treaties, one might ask why we focus on treaties in the first place, rather than norms more broadly.

---

[8] The text of the Swiss reservation to art. 59 of the Istanbul Convention can be found here (Renewal of reservations contained in a letter from the Permanent Representative of Switzerland, dated 14 November 2022): https://www.coe.int/en/web/conventions/full-list?module=declarations-by-treaty&numSte=210&codeNature=0.

2.3.4 Why Treaties (Rather than Legal Norms)?

We concentrate on obligations from treaty law. Contemporary international law operates through treaties, customary law, and general principles but also through a bewildering array of instruments that cannot easily be subsumed with one of the above categories (such as decisions of international organisations, sometimes decisions taken by bodies of a hybrid nature, 'soft' or informal law, etc.). Obligations expressed in legally binding treaties express most clearly the ambitions of international law towards domestic actors and thus lend themselves to our purposes. Moreover, the focus on treaties is warranted for feasibility considerations. As in Beth Simmons' study on *Mobilizing for Human Rights*, '[n]orms are too broad a concept' for what we have in mind for this study and 'treaties are understood by domestic and international audiences as especially clear statements of intended behavior' (Simmons, 2012, p. 7). The choice to focus on treaties is the starting point but we will consider the broader normative landscape surrounding the treaty obligations which we examine. For instance, the mentioned explanatory report of the Istanbul Convention, a document prepared by the treaty secretariat, is non-binding but some interview partners shared with us how the report is important for their work. This observation indicates that legal bindingness and the wider normative context can influence the ease with which subnational actors use human rights treaties. Moreover, and maybe most importantly, studying uses of a treaty and political authorities' engagement with it implies taking into account not only the norms and obligations, but also the treaty as a whole: the reference to the treaty can be used as an argument and a legitimation to take policy measures or to change the policy paradigm, or it can be a cognitive resource to understand and (re)frame a public problem and a policy. In short, this choice allows us to consider not only the direct uses and implementation of norms, but also the more diffuse mobilisations and effects of the treaty in policy processes.

In the last section of this chapter, we will address the data collection.

2.4 The Collected Datasets

To observe the uses of the Istanbul Convention and the CRPD, we collected two complementary qualitative datasets.

2.4.1 Desk Research on Official Sources Related to the Treaties

First, we conducted desk research to collect official sources on both treaties at the federal, inter-cantonal and cantonal level. Following Donald and Speck's invitation (Donald & Speck, 2020), we took a processual approach analysing the political and bureaucratic processes through which the treaties affect cantonal policymaking. Our approach aims at reconstructing the existing narratives about policy processes related to the implementation of these treaties, identifying the different uses of the treaties in Swiss cantons, as well as the mechanisms and patterns through which subnational political authorities engage with them.

To identify these processes, uses and mechanisms, we first collected and analysed the federal government dispatches accompanying federal bills, governmental reports and official administrative documentation related to the Istanbul Convention and the CRPD, and their intended implementation at the federal and cantonal levels. Then, we collected and analysed official documents at the cantonal level, including parliamentary interventions, responses of cantonal government and parliamentary debates. We did so in 25 cantons (out of 26) for the Istanbul Convention and in 19 cantons for the CRPD (see Table 2.1). We also collected the documents and official reactions related to the evaluation processes by the Council of Europe Expert Group on Action against Violence against Women and Domestic Violence (GREVIO) and the UN Committee on the Rights of Persons with Disabilities (UNCRPD), both in 2022. Finally, we observed the interactive dialogue between the UN Committee on the Rights of Persons with Disabilities (the United Nations supervisory body concerning the CRPD) and the delegation of Switzerland during the review of Switzerland in March 2022 at the United Nations in Geneva. These international supervisory mechanisms produce non-binding recommendations on the implementation of the relevant treaty by the state. They base their assessment on a report produced by the state party, and information submitted by civil society, as well as other available documents. The timeframe of our research begins with the documentation leading to the ratification of these two treaties—2014 for the CRPD and 2017 for the IC—and finishes at the end of 2022.

Table 2.1 Characteristics of Swiss cantons (at time of data collection) and cantons included in desk research

Cantons	Language(s)	Population (2021)	Legislature	Strength of the left in Government[a]	Strength of the left in Parliament[b]	IC	CRPD
Aargau	G	694 871	2020–2024	Weak	Quite weak	X	
Appenzell Ausserrhoden	G	54 713	2019–2023	Weak	Weak	X	X
Appenzell Innerrhoden	G	16 078	2019–2023	n/a[c]	n/a		
Basel-Landschaft	G	288 747	2019–2023	Strong	Strong	X	X
Basel-Stadt	G	191 395	2021–2025	Strong	Strong	X	X
Bern	G, F	1 028 269	2022–2026	Strong	Quite strong	X	X
Fribourg	F, G	323 919	2022–2026	Quite weak	Quite strong	X	X
Genève	F	483 503	2018–2023	Strong	Quite strong	X	X
Glarus	G	40 370	2018–2022	Null	Quite weak	X	X
Graubünden	G, R, I	198 347	2018–2022	Weak	Weak	X	
Jura	F	72 712	2021–2025	Strong	Strong	X	X
Luzern	G	413 128	2019–2023	Null	Quite weak	X	X
Neuchâtel	F	173 333	2017–2021	Very strong	Strong	X	X
Nidwald	G	43 254	2018–2022	Null	Weak	X	X
Obwald	G	37 902	2018–2022	Null	Quite weak	X	
Schaffhausen	G	82 537	2021–2025	Strong	Quite strong	X	X
Schwyz	G	161 353	2020–2024	Null	Weak	X	X
Solothurn	G	276 142	2021–2025	Strong	Quite strong	X	
St.Gallen	G	511 609	2021–2025	Quite weak	Quite weak	X	X
Thurgau	G	282 421	2020–2024	Weak	Quite weak	X	
Ticino	I	346 433	2019–2023	Weak	Quite weak	X	
Uri	G	36 238	2020–2024	Weak	Weak	X	
Valais	F, G	346 562	2021–2025	Weak	Quite weak	X	
Vaud	F	806 035	2017–2022	Very strong	Strong	X	X
Zug	G	127 680	2018–2022	Null	Quite weak	X	X
Zurich	G	1 537 408	2019–2023	Strong	Quite strong	X	X

[a] % of members from left parties: <21 weak, 21–29 quite weak, 30–39 quite strong, 40–49 strong, >50 very strong

[b] % of members from left parties: <21 weak, 21–29 quite weak, 30–39 quite strong, 40–49 strong, >50 very strong

[c] In Appenzell Innerrhoden, most members of the government and parliament are not affiliated to a party

F French; *G* German; *I* Italian; *R* Romansh

2.4.2 Semi-Structured Interviews

To build our second dataset, we conducted 65 semi-structured interviews with 69 persons who were somehow involved in the implementation of the Istanbul Convention or the CRPD, to understand how these actors use the treaties. Our interview partners can be categorised into the following groups of actors:

- four interviewees are or were members of the federal administration (Federal Office of Gender Equality; Federal Office of Justice; Federal Department of International Law; Federal Office of Equality for Persons with Disabilities);
- 27 members of cantonal administrations responsible for the implementation of the Istanbul Convention in 18 cantons,[9] respectively of the CRPD in four cantons[10];
- 34 members of cantonal parliaments in four cantons[11];
- two members of a cantonal government;
- five members of civil society organisations and/or academic experts involved in cantonal legislative processes.[12]

For these semi-structured interviews, we created an interview guide with main questions and follow-up (sub)questions. We first asked the persons to present their roles, tasks and functions, as well as the organisation(s) for which they work.

Second, we asked the interviewees to describe and explain, from their point of view, the general situation on the implementation of the relevant treaty in the canton and/or (if relevant) the processes in which they were involved, such as drafting a parliamentary intervention, participating in a parliamentary commission working on a law reform, drafting a law project, drafting proposals to implement the treaty (e.g. an action plan against domestic violence), etc. We paid particular attention to what actors concretely do, to the different stages of the process, to the actors who are involved, to the points of tension between them, and to the role of the convention in the process.

Third, when examining the different stages of the policy process, we asked about specific uses of the relevant treaty: how did the interviewees come to know that this treaty existed, how did they understand it and decide to use it (or not) in drafting a parliamentary intervention, a law project, or an action plan, and how did they come to write an intervention, or to propose a legislative reform? Numerous sub-questions aimed at exploring which actors used

---

[9] Aargau, Basel-Landschaft, Bern, Fribourg, Geneva, Glarus, Graubünden, Jura, Lucerne, Neuchâtel, St. Gallen, Schaffhausen, Schwyz, Solothurn, Thurgau, Valais, Vaud and Zurich.

[10] Jura, Neuchâtel, Valais and Vaud.

[11] Geneva, Neuchâtel, Schwyz and Zurich.

[12] Some persons interviewed had several different roles in the process and are counted two and three times.

the treaty and how exactly, with which goals, and with which effects on the process. We also asked specific questions about the roles of other actors, such as the different political authorities involved and the points of tension between them.

Fourth, we asked questions aiming at analysing the relationships between the interviewee and the treaty and, more generally, international law. In our view, the notion of relationships to international law is close to legal consciousness taken in a broad sense.[13] Thus, we asked questions about how they came to know international law, how they work with it and use it in their role (as a member of a cantonal parliament, or as a cantonal official), how obligatory they perceive human rights treaties to be, and what the treaty has changed (for them and in the cantonal policymaking). We also asked questions regarding implementation of international law in general (how it happens, and how they believe it should happen), and its place in cantonal policy processes.

Fifth, we asked questions about how they perceive their role (of parliamentarians or of cantonal officials), how they perform it, what are their areas of specialty, how did they learn their role, etc.

Finally, we asked questions about their biographical and socio-professional trajectory and their political commitments. We translated all our interview excerpts and quotes of documents from French or from German.

2.4.3 Selection of Four Cantons for In-Depth Analysis

Switzerland consists of 26 cantons. We managed to collect and analyse official sources, and to interview key members of several cantonal administrations (see Table 2.1). As it would exceed the scope of this book to study processes in a large number of cantons, we selected a sample of four diverse cantons for in-depth analysis. We notably focused our interviews with members of cantonal parliaments on this sample, which enabled us to interview parliamentarians from different political parties in each canton. We selected cantons to maximise variations in the most relevant contextual variables, as it is warranted for qualitative research (Plümper et al., 2019). Therefore, we decided on a list of four cantons considered as diverse, notably in terms of size, language, degree of urbanisation and parliament's resource capacity, professionalisation and political position (in green in Table 2.1). The objective is to maximise the chances of observing different implementation processes and uses of human rights treaties. We identified Geneva as a 'most likely case' in terms of implementation: a large French-speaking and urban canton with a resourceful,

---

[13] 'Legal consciousness refers to the ways in which people experience, understand, and act in relation to law. It comprises both cognition and behavior, both the ideologies and the practices of people as they navigate their way through situations in which law could play a role. Legal consciousness does not simply refer to legal awareness, nor is it meant to measure knowledge—or ignorance—of the law. Indeed, some legal consciousness research demonstrates the extent to which people do not invoke or think about the law at all—or perceive it to be irrelevant' (Chua, 2019, p. 336).

strongly professionalised[14] and politically heterogenous parliament with rather strong left parties and uniquely strong relationships with international organisations. By contrast, Schwyz is our 'least likely case': a small German-speaking rural canton with a weakly professionalised, strongly right-wing parliaments and governments. We added two intermediary cases: Neuchâtel (a small French-speaking canton with a weakly professionalised parliament and strong left parties) and Zurich (a large German-speaking canton with a strongly professionalised, right-wing parliament but the presence of rather strong left parties).

Whenever we refer to cantons, we refer to the subnational units of the Swiss federal state. We thus use the term 'subnational actor' as a synonym of actors situated at the cantonal level, and we do not further distinguish lower subnational entities. The cantons are composed of municipalities that also have some autonomy (and this level of autonomy varies from one canton to another). For reasons of simplicity, we make abstraction of the municipal level. This comes, unfortunately, at the disadvantage of ignoring the recent research on the role of cities in implementing international law and protecting human rights (Aust & Nijman, 2021; Frei, 2022; Grigolo, 2019; Nijman et al., 2022). That said, we are indirectly able to consider initiatives arising, e.g. in a city given that such initiatives, at least in Switzerland, invariably impact one or the other actor at the cantonal level.

Table 2.1 presents the 26 Swiss cantons. Switzerland has four national languages: German (G), French (F), Italian (I), and Romansh (R). The table highlights that Swiss cantons are very diverse in terms of population, ranging from 16,000 inhabitants (Appenzell Innerrhoden) to 1.5 million (Zurich). The table also outlines the strength of the left in cantonal parliaments and governments in the legislature on which we focused our analysis, using the data of the Swiss Federal Statistical Office. All this information helped us to select specific cantons for in-depth analysis and for our comparative analysis of the cantons.

2.4.4 *Analysing the Datasets from Different Perspectives*

The creation of these two datasets enabled us to have a clear and critical view of the ratification and implementation processes of the Istanbul Convention and the CRPD in Switzerland (Chapter 3). We then analysed this data using thematic content analysis and interpretative qualitative methods (Dubois, 2009; Yanow, 2017). The first step was the identification of themes and patterns across the documents and the transcripts of the interviews with

---

[14] This is relative as cantonal parliaments are non-professional. Members of the Geneva parliament spend around 40% of a full-time equivalent for politics, the highest proportion in Switzerland. The Swiss average is around 20% of a full-time equivalent. In the canton of Schwyz, this percentage is around 10% (Bundi et al., 2017).

the software MAXQDA. We started from the lived experience of our interviewees to analyse how they came to know about international treaties, how they understand them. We then retraced and reconstructed policy processes related to treaties: their impulse, the mechanisms through which treaties played a role, the role of the various actors involved, and the outputs. This enabled us to understand the uses that subnational actors make of the treaties. The analysis of interview transcripts also enabled us to obtain very specific information on cantonal contexts, which added some flesh to the desk research we carried out on cantonal characteristics (see Table 2.1). We also analysed personal characteristics and eventually associated contextual features and characteristics of interviewees with specific uses of treaties (Chapter 4). Taking a step back in order to examine the broader picture, these elements helped us to understand through which mechanisms and patterns the subnational political authorities engage with international treaties, and to classify these engagements (Chapter 5). Our hope is that by being as transparent as possible about the qualitative data and its limits, we will provide sufficient evidence to illustrate how subnational actors, even sometimes single individuals, are active agents of the realities of human rights on the ground and can make a positive difference towards the engagement of political authorities.

References

Abbott, K. W., Levi-Faur, D., & Snidal, D. (2017). Introducing Regulatory Intermediaries. *The ANNALS of the American Academy of Political and Social Science, 670*(1), 6–13.

Aust, H., & Nijman, J. (Eds.). (2021). *International Law and Cities*. Edward Elgar.

Baudot, P.-Y. (2018). Layering Rights: The Case of Disability Policies in France (2006–2016). *Social Policy & Society, 17*(1), 117–131. https://doi.org/10.1017/S1474746417000392

Beach, D., & Pedersen, R. B. (2019). Process-Tracing Methods. *University of Michigan Press*. https://doi.org/10.1093/OBO/9780199743292-0227

Bennett, A., & Checkel, J. T. (2012). Process Tracing: From Philosophical Roots to Best Practices. *Process Tracing in the Social Sciences*, 3–38.

Billows, S., Butcher, L., & Pélisse, J. (2019). Introduction: The Microfoundations of Legal Intermediation in Organizational Contexts. *Studies in Law, Politics, and Society, 81*, 1–9. https://doi.org/10.1108/S1059-433720190000081001

Bundi, P., Eberli, D., & Bütikofer, S. (2017). Between Occupation and Politics: Legislative Professionalization in the Swiss Cantons. *Swiss Political Science Review, 23*(1), 1–20. https://doi.org/10.1111/spsr.12228

Butcher, L. (2019). "Companies Can Do Better Than the Law": Securing Rights for Minorities as an Insider Activist in French Corporation. *Studies in Law, Politics and Society, 81*, 11–44.

Chua, L., & Engel, D. (2019). Legal Consciousness Reconsidered. *Annual Review of Law and Social Science, 15*, 335–354.

De Vido, S. (2017). The Ratification of the Council of Europe Istanbul Convention by the EU: A Step Forward in the Protection of Women from Violence in the European Legal System. *European Journal of Legal Studies, 9*(2), 69–102.

Donald, A., & Speck, A.-K. (2020). The Dynamics of Domestic Human Rights Implementation: Lessons from Qualitative Research in Europe. *Journal of Human Rights Practice, 12*(1), 48–70. https://doi.org/10.1093/jhuman/huaa007

Dubois, V. (2009). Towards a Critical Policy Ethnography: The 'Undeserving Poor' and the New Welfare State. *Critical Policy Studies, 3*(2), 219–237.

Frei, N. (2022). La mise en oeuvre de la Convention relative aux droits de l'enfant par les villes et les communes suisses. *Swiss Review International and European Law, 4*, 585–615.

Garth, B. G. (2006). Introduction: Taking New Legal Realism to Transnational Issues and Institutions. *Law & Social Inquiry, 31*(4), 939–945. https://doi.org/10.1111/j.1747-4469.2006.00040.x

George, A. L., & Bennett, A. (2005). *Case Studies and Theory Development in the Social Sciences*. MIT Press.

Grans, L. (2018). The Istanbul Convention and the Positive Obligation to Prevent Violence. *Human Rights Law Review, 18*(1), 133–155. https://doi.org/10.1093/hrlr/ngx041

Gray, G., & Pélisse, J. (2019). Frontline Workers and the Role of Legal and Regulatory Intermediaries. *Sciences Po LIEPP Working Paper*, (94), 1–17.

Grigolo, M. (2019). *The Human Rights City: New York, San Francisco, Barcelona*. Routledge.

Haglund, L., & Stryker, R. (2015). *Closing the Rights Gap: From Human Rights to Social Transformation*. University of California Press.

Heyer, K. (2015). *Rights Enabled: The Disability Revolutionl, from the US, to Germany and Japan, to the United Nations*. University of Michigan Press.

Holtermann, J. V. H., & Madsen, M. R. (2021). European New Legal Realism: Towards a Basic Science of Law. In S. Talesh, H. Klug, & E. Mertz (Eds.), *Research Handbook on Modern Legal Realism* (pp. 67–81). Edward Elgar Publishing.

Kaempfer, C. (2023). *Les mécanismes de mise en oeuvre du droit international par les cantons suisses: études de cas dans les domaines des droits humains et des accords bilatéraux Suisse-UE*. Sui generis.

Kapiszewski, D., & Taylor, M. M. (2013). Compliance: Conceptualizing, Measuring, and Explaining Adherence to Judicial Rulings. *Law & Social Inquiry, 38*(4), 803–835.

Klug, H., & Merry, S. (Eds.). (2016). *The New Legal Realism: Studying Law Globally*. Cambridge University Press.

Krommendijk, J. (2018). National Parliaments: Obstacles or Aid to the Impact of International Human Rights Bodies? In M. Wind (Ed.), *International Courts and Domestic Politics* (pp. 227–261). Cambridge University Press.

Ku, C., William, H., Stewart, D., & Diehl, P. (2019). Even Some International Law Is Local: Implementation of Treaties Through Subnational Mechanisms. *Virginia Journal of International Law, 60*(1), 105–158.

Lejeune, A., & Ringelheim, J. (2019). Workers with Disabilities Between Legal Changes and Persisting Exclusion: How Contradictory Rights Shape Legal Mobilization. *Law & Society Review, 53*(4), 983–1015. https://doi.org/10.1111/lasr.12439

Levitt, P., & Merry, S. (2009). Vernacularization on the Ground: Local Uses of Global Women's Rights in Peru, China, India and the United States. *Global Networks, 9*(4), 441–461. https://doi.org/10.1111/j.1471-0374.2009.00263.x

Maggetti, M. (2021). L'échelon international-transnational de l'action publique. In S. Jacob & N. Schiffino (Eds.), *Traité en analyse des politiques publiques* (pp. 849–876). Larcier Bruylant.

Maggetti, M., & Trein, P. (2019). Multilevel Governance and Problem-Solving: Towards a Dynamic Theory of Multilevel Policy-Making? *Public Administration, 97*(2), 355–369.

McQuigg, R. J. A. (2012). What Potential does the Council of Europe Convention on Violence against Women Hold as Regards Domestic Violence? *The International Journal of Human Rights, 16*(7), 947–962. https://doi.org/10.1080/13642987.2011.638288

Merry, S. E. (2006a). *Human Rights and Gender Violence: Translating International Law into Local Justice*. University of Chicago Press.

Merry, S. E. (2006b). New Legal Realism and the Ethnography of Transnational Law. *Law & Social Inquiry, 31*(4), 975–995. https://doi.org/10.1111/j.1747-4469.2006.00042.x

Merry, S. E. (2006c). Transnational Human Rights and Local Activism: Mapping the Middle. *American Anthropologist, 108*(1), 38–51.

Merry, S. E., & Levitt, P. (2017). The Vernacularization of Women's Human Rights. In S. Hopgood, J. Snyder, & L. Vinjamuri (Eds.), *Human Rights Futures* (pp. 213–236). Cambridge University Press.

Miaz, J., Niederhauser, M., & Maggetti, M. (2024). From International Law to Subnational Practices: The Roles of Intermediaries in Translating the Istanbul Convention in Swiss Cantons. *Regulation & Governance*, 1–19. https://doi.org/10.1111/rego.12523

Milet, M. (2020). Parliament in the Policymaking Process: Toward a Sociology of Law-Making. In C. Benoit & O. Rozenberg (Eds.), *Handbook of Parliamentary Studies: Interdisciplinary Approaches to Legislatures* (pp. 445–464). Edward Elgar Publishing.

Nijman, J., Oomen, B., Durmus, E., Miellet, S., & Roodenburg, L. (Eds.). (2022). *Urban Politics of Human Rights*. Routledge.

Oliver, M. (2009). *Understanding Disability: From Theory to Practice*. Palgrave Macmillan (2nd ed.).

Pegram, T. (2017). Regulatory Stewardship and Intermediation: Lessons from Human Rights Governance. *The ANNALS of the American Academy of Political and Social Science, 670*(1), 225–244.

Pélisse, J. (2019). Varieties of Legal Intermediaries: When Non-Legal Professionals Act as Legal Intermediaries. *Studies in Law, Politics and Society, 81*, 101–128.

Plümper, T., Troeger, V., & Neumayer, E. (2019). Case Selection and Causal Inferences in Qualitative Comparative Research. *PLoS ONE, 14*(7), 1–18. https://doi.org/10.1371/journal.pone.0219727

Quinn, G., & Flynn, E. (2012). Transatlantic Borrowings: The Past and Future of EU Non-Discrimination Law and Policy on the Ground of Disability. *The American Journal of Comparative Law, 60*(1), 23–48. https://doi.org/10.5131/AJCL.2011.0023

Revillard, A. (2018). Vulnerable Rights: The Incomplete Realization of Disability Social Rights in France. *Social Sciences, 7*(6), 88–104. https://doi.org/10.3390/socsci7060088

Revillard, A. (2019). Realizing the Right to Access in France: Between Implementation and Activation. *Law & Society Review*, 53(4), 950–982. https://doi.org/10.1111/lasr.12434

Revillard, A. (2023). *Fragile Rights. Disability, Public Policy, and Social Change*. Bristol University Press.

Sasseville, N., Maurice, P., Montminy, L., Hassan, G., & St-Pierre, É. (2022). Cumulative Contexts of Vulnerability to Intimate Partner Violence Among Women With Disabilities, Elderly Women, and Immigrant Women: Prevalence, Risk Factors, Explanatory Theories, and Prevention. *Trauma, Violence, & Abuse*, 23(1), 88–100. https://doi.org/10.1177/1524838020925773

Schmid, E. (2015). The Identification and Role of International Legislative Duties in a Contested Area: Must Switzerland Legislate in Relation to «Business and Human Rights»? *Swiss Review International and European Law*, (4), 563–589.

Schmid, E. (2019). How Upper Levels Strive to Influence Law-Making at the Lower Levels and Why Lower Levels Can't Have Cake and Eat It. In P. Popelier, H. Xanthaki, F. Uhlmann, T. Silveira Joāp, & W. Robinson (Eds.), *Lawmaking in Multi-level Settings Legislative Challenges in Federal Systems and the European Union* (pp. 43–67). Hart/Nomos.

Shaffer, G. (2012). Transnational Legal Process and State Change. *Law & Social Inquiry*, 37(02), 229–264. https://doi.org/10.1111/j.1747-4469.2011.01265.x

Shaffer, G. (2015). The New Legal Realist Approach to International Law. *Leiden Journal of International Law*, 28(2), 189–210. https://doi.org/10.1017/S0922156515000035

Shaffer, G. (2016). New Legal Realism and International Law. In H. Klug & S. E. Merry (Eds.), *The New Legal Realism: Studying Law Globally* (Vol. 2, pp. 145–159). Cambridge University Press.

Simmons, B. (2012). *Mobilizing for Human Rights: International Law in Domestic Politics*. Cambridge University Press.

Talesh, S., & Pélisse, J. (2019). How Legal Intermediaries Facilitate or Inhibit Social Change. *Studies in Law, Politics and Society*, 79, 111–145.

Talesh, S. A., Mertz, E., & Klug, H. (2021). Introduction to the Research Handbook on Modern Legal Realism. In S. A. Talesh, E. Mertz, & H. Klug (Eds.), *Research Handbook on Modern Legal Realism* (pp. 1–20). Edward Elgar Publishing. https://www.elgaronline.com/view/edcoll/9781788117760/9781788117760.xml

Thomann, E. (2015). Customizing Europe: Transposition as Bottom-up Implementation. *Journal of European Public Policy*, 22(10), 1368–1387. https://doi.org/10.1080/13501763.2015.1008554

Thomann, E., & Sager, F. (2017). Moving Beyond Legal Compliance: Innovative Approaches to EU Multilevel Implementation. *Journal of European Public Policy*, 24(9), 1253–1268. https://doi.org/10.1080/13501763.2017.1314541

Thomann, E., Trein, P., & Maggetti, M. (2019). What's the Problem? Multilevel Governance and Problem-Solving. *European Policy Analysis*, 5(1), 37–57. https://doi.org/10.1002/epa2.1062

Vincent, F. (2019). A Multi-Level Approach to Legal Intermediation: The Case of the 12-Hour Work Derogation in French Public Hospitals. *Studies in Law, Politics and Society*, 81, 69–99.

Wyttenbach, J. (2018). Systemic and Structural Factors Relating to Quality and Equality of Human Rights Implementation in Federal States. *International Human Rights Law Review*, 7(1), 43–81. https://doi.org/10.1163/22131035-00701002

Yanow, D. (2017). Qualitative-Interpretive Methods in Policy Research. In F. Fischer, G. Miller, & M. S. Sidney (Eds.), *Handbook of Public Policy Analysis* (pp. 405–415). Taylor & Francis.

Open Access This chapter is licensed under the terms of the Creative Commons Attribution 4.0 International License (http://creativecommons.org/licenses/by/4.0/), which permits use, sharing, adaptation, distribution and reproduction in any medium or format, as long as you give appropriate credit to the original author(s) and the source, provide a link to the Creative Commons license and indicate if changes were made.

The images or other third party material in this chapter are included in the chapter's Creative Commons license, unless indicated otherwise in a credit line to the material. If material is not included in the chapter's Creative Commons license and your intended use is not permitted by statutory regulation or exceeds the permitted use, you will need to obtain permission directly from the copyright holder.

CHAPTER 3

Shaping the Uses of a Treaty Through Ratification and Implementation Procedures

Abstract After being signed by a state, international human rights treaties must be formally ratified and then implemented. What happens before and during the ratification may influence the future uses of—and engagements with—human rights treaties and different mechanisms are employed to try to spur engagement and implementation. Through case studies of the Istanbul Convention and the UN Convention on the Rights of Persons with Disabilities, we demonstrate, first, how a government may try to shape the preferences of its subnational units through the pre-ratification procedure. Second, we show how federal, inter-cantonal and cantonal actors employ or develop 'domestic implementation mechanisms' to orient the engagement of subnational units. While these mechanisms sometimes stem from the federal or inter-cantonal level, they can also arise from actions taken at the subnational level, unfolding in a bottom-up process.

Keywords Federalism · Human rights treaties · Implementation mechanisms · Treaty ratification · Switzerland

3.1 Introduction

To become effective, international human rights treaties first need to be ratified and implemented by state parties. It is useful to scrutinise the ratification of a treaty and the mechanisms employed with a view to implement it because these processes will orient the future uses of—and engagements with—a treaty. Beyond explaining the Swiss constitutional framework relating to international treaties, this chapter aims to outline the procedures and mechanisms that will influence how subnational political actors view and use a treaty. We will show that even the understudied pre-ratification procedure is worth being researched for this purpose. Indeed, as Simmons demonstrated, a government's support for treaty ratification may be based on its domestic actors' preferences (and notably those of its subnational units) rather than on the content of the treaty (Simmons, 2012). Audrey Comstock aptly observed how the ratification of a human rights treaty is just one aspect of a state's commitment to the human rights issues contained in the treaty (Comstock, 2021, pp. 23–45), and the ratification alone does not reveal yet whether and how the political authorities of a state intend to engage with the treaty. Rather, pushing the analysis further, we argue that the pre-ratification procedure constitutes an opportunity for the government to influence the preferences of actors within subnational units, which would consequently shape the later uses of a treaty. As explained before, no standard procedure exists for implementing human rights treaties. However, different 'domestic implementation mechanisms' (Kaempfer, 2023) are used by the actors who want to facilitate an engagement of subnational units with international treaties, potentially leading to implementation. Through a classification of these mechanisms in four categories (namely, sanctions, rewards, awareness-raising and co-operation), we show how they aim to orient the ways in which human rights treaties are later used, engaged with and implemented.

This chapter first presents the literature relating to the ratification of international human rights treaties, and to the notion of 'domestic implementation mechanisms'. The chapter goes on to present the procedure for the ratification of international treaties and the available implementation mechanisms in Switzerland and then highlights the ratification and implementation mechanisms of our two case studies: the Istanbul Convention and the UN Convention on the Rights of Persons with Disabilities (CRPD). This enables us to identify and categorise the mechanisms used for the implementation of these treaties and discuss their implications.

3.2 Theoretical Framework on Ratification and Implementation

From a legal point of view, before the political authorities of a state (including subnational units) use—and sometimes engage with—an international treaty, it needs to be ratified. As we will show, this ratification procedure may already influence the way in which subnational units use the treaty. We will also explain how, in federal states, 'domestic implementation mechanisms' are sometimes developed at federal, inter-cantonal or cantonal level to orient subnational units in their uses of the treaty.

3.2.1 The Ratification of Treaties

In her book *Mobilizing for Human Rights*, Simmons (2012) explains that the 'negotiation and ratification [of treaties] reflect the power, organization, and aspirations of the governments that negotiate and sign them, the legislatures that ratify them, and the groups that lobby on their behalf' (Simmons, 2012, p. 12). She also puts the emphasis on the influence that domestic institutions (and notably their subnational units) might have on a government's support for the ratification of a treaty:

> Because governments sometimes anticipate that ratification will impose political costs that they are not ready to bear, they sometimes self-screen. [...] The point is this: Two governments with similar values may appear on opposite sides of the ratification divide because of their domestic institutions rather than their preferences for the content of the treaty itself. Treaties may act as screens, but domestic institutions can do so as well. (Simmons, 2012, p. 13)

We also believe that a government's support for ratification may depend on the stance of their domestic institutions as well as on the content of the treaty. In this chapter, we wish to push the analysis further and show how the ratification procedure enables the government to influence domestic institutions. A government may for instance use this procedure to downplay the implications of a ratification. Moreover, we argue that the ratification procedure also influences how domestic institutions later use—and engage with—the treaty.

3.2.2 The Implementation of Treaties

According to the principle of *pacta sunt servanda*, once an international treaty has been ratified, it is binding upon the contracting parties and they must faithfully perform the obligations it contains.[1] The corollary of this principle is that a state cannot invoke the legislative procedures of its internal law to justify the non-performance of an obligation arising from a treaty.[2] Except for this general rule prohibiting states from invoking internal legal issues to avoid complying with international law and the general obligation to fulfil its commitments, international law does not contain any general provisions regarding its implementation (Cassese, 2005, p. 219). This gives each state considerable freedom as to how it fulfils its international obligations domestically (Cassese, 2005, p. 219; Denza, 2018, p. 386).

Given this freedom, several states have developed their own 'domestic implementation mechanisms' (Kaempfer, 2021). According to Simmons, compliance with international human rights treaties is mainly the result of

---

[1] Art. 26 of the Vienna Convention on the Law of Treaties, 1155 UNTS 331, 23 May 1969 (entered into force 27 January 1980).

[2] Art. 27 of the Vienna Convention on the Law of Treaties, 1155 UNTS 331, 23 May 1969 (entered into force 27 January 1980).

mechanisms operating at a domestic level (Simmons, 2012, p. 126). De Beco also thinks that domestic non-judicial mechanisms (national human rights institutions, human rights indicators, human rights impact assessments and national human right action plans) are essential to implement human rights (De Beco, 2010, p. 3). More recently, different authors also recognised the decisive role of domestic mechanisms in the field of internal enforcement of decisions issued by supranational bodies (Donald & Speck, 2020, p. 67; Murray, 2020, p. 1). Such mechanisms are particularly important to determine which state actor is responsible and how implementation should be co-ordinated (Murray & De Vos, 2020, p. 29). Other scholars mention the importance of governmental focal points within the administration and parliamentary human rights committees to bridge 'the implementation gap between commitments and reality' (Jensen et al., 2019, p. 165 f.).

In this book, 'domestic implementation mechanisms' are regarded as facilitators for subnational units to engage with human rights treaties and, potentially, to facilitate implementation. The function of such mechanisms is to influence or produce an outcome. Yet, the outcome (implementation or lack thereof) is not decisive for a measure to qualify as a mechanism. Moreover, 'domestic implementation mechanisms' are exclusively internal. This excludes international implementation mechanisms such as regional courts, UN mechanisms (such as treaty bodies or the Universal Periodic Review) or other international monitoring and communications procedures. Such mechanisms can be very useful to help domestic (including subnational) authorities interpret and engage with international obligations. In particular, international reports or decisions can be strategically used by civil society or legislators to push a legislative project. While we take such documents into account when analysing the uses of and the engagement with international treaties in the cantons, we do not study the effect of these mechanisms on subnational actors in Swiss cantons. Indeed, this book studies how the engagement comes about within the domestic legal system and how subnational actors use human rights treaties. It does not seek to understand e.g. how UN bodies interpret these treaties. This approach follows a trend in international literature to focus on local actors of implementation (Jensen et al., 2019, p. 165).

Based on these criteria, several measures can be qualified as 'domestic implementation mechanisms': reports, structures, guides, dissemination of 'good practices', monitoring, scientific support, subventions, models, etc. But what about pre-existing structural or political conditions (political agenda, institutional characteristics of parliament, size of the canton, etc.) which also influence the implementation process? While they certainly play an important role, such influences cannot be described as mechanisms. These conditions rather 'create both opportunities and obstacles for pro-implementation actors' (Donald & Speck, 2020, p. 67). However, they do not directly aim at encouraging implementation. These factors and conditions, which may limit or enable engagement with international treaties, are discussed in Chapter 5.

Finally, we only include mechanisms that originate with actors involved in the policy process. Such actors are either *de jure* supposed to engage with the treaty (e.g. Federal government, subnational parliaments and subnational governments) or brought into the process by those who are (e.g. external experts mandated by the parliament).

3.3 Ratification and Implementation of International Treaties in Switzerland

This section describes how treaties are ratified and which types of 'domestic implementation mechanisms' already exist in the Swiss legal order. It highlights how these procedures and mechanisms can orient the way a treaty is used in subnational policy processes.

3.3.1 The (Pre-)Ratification Procedure

Before ratifying an international treaty, the Swiss government (the Federal Council) has to organise a consultation procedure,[3] sometimes referred to as a 'pre-parliamentary consultation procedure', which 'has the aim of allowing the cantons, political parties and interested groups to participate in the shaping of opinion and the decision-making process of the Confederation'.[4] It is mandatory for the adoption of certain legal instruments—notably for international law agreements that are subject to a referendum—and for projects that 'significantly affect individual cantons or all the cantons'.[5]

The relevant department of the Swiss government thus sends a 'Preliminary project and explanatory report' to the cantons, political parties and interested groups. This document is supposed to present the treaty and explain all its implications—notably which provisions fall into cantonal competences and what will be the consequences on the finances and personnel situation of the cantons. This document also provides the Swiss government with an opportunity to interpret the Convention and orient the implementation in case of ratification. For instance, if the government states that Switzerland already fully complies with a treaty, it is likely that most cantonal authorities will then take that for granted and not look at the treaty in detail. In practice, we observe that the government generally speaks deferentially in these documents: they are never very directive towards the cantons and often understate the measures that they might have to take in case of ratification. This

---

[3] This is foreseen by Article 147 of the Swiss Federal Constitution: 'The Cantons, the political parties and interested groups shall be invited to express their views when preparing important legislation or other projects of substantial impact as well as in relation to significant international treaties'. Before that, cantons may also participate in the negotiations of international treaties if their powers are affected, according to Article 55 al. 3 of the Swiss Federal Constitution.

[4] Article 2 of the 2005 Federal Act on the Consultation Procedure.

[5] Article 3 of the 2005 Federal Act on the Consultation Procedure.

is probably because (1) the federal government does not feel legitimate to tell the cantons what they have to do in view of Swiss federalist division of competences and/or (2) the government willingly understates the required measures in order to ensure subnational support for the treaty. As demonstrated by Simmons (Simmons, 2012), a government's support for ratification may depend on the structure of its domestic institutions and on the political context (and notably its subnational units) rather than on the content of the treaty. We show that the consultation procedure enables the government to influence domestic institutions and notably to make appear the implications of ratification minor.

Cantonal constitutions generally foresee that governmental authorities are consulted during this process (Nuspliger, 2006). Usually, cantonal governments then consult the relevant services of their administration. This procedure provides cantons with an opportunity to comment and support or oppose the ratification of new international treaties by Switzerland.

Following the consultation procedure, the Swiss government requests the Swiss parliament to approve new treaties (according to Article 166 al. 2 of the Federal Constitution, the Swiss parliament has to 'approve international treaties, with the exception of those that are concluded by the Federal Council [the Swiss government] under a statutory provision or an international treaty'). The Federal Council sends this request along with its 'Message', which is published in the 'Federal Gazette'. The Message is largely based on the Preliminary project and explanatory report used for the consultation procedure, but it also mentions the replies received during that procedure. Once the Swiss parliament approves the treaty, the Federal Council then usually ratifies the treaty and announces when it will enter into force. The treaty is then published in the Official Compendium of Swiss Federal Law.

3.3.2 *The Implementation Procedure*

The Swiss legal framework for the implementation of international law is minimalist. It lays down general principles relating to the implementation of international law but does not establish concrete rules. Therefore, in practice the implementation of international treaties in Switzerland takes various forms, as we will see in the following sections. Sometimes, inter-cantonal conferences play an important role in the cantonal implementation of international treaties. Inter-cantonal conferences are composed of members of various cantonal executives who co-ordinate between the cantons around thematic issues. This was the case for the implementation of the Istanbul Convention. At other times, independent groups of experts can act as driving forces in the implementation process, as the case for the Convention on the Rights of Persons with Disabilities.

In the absence of a well-established framework for the implementation of international treaties, several 'domestic implementation mechanisms' have been developed by different actors to implement international treaties

(Kaempfer, 2023). Based on a study of a broad range of international law instruments, including both international human rights treaties and European Union law, Constance Kaempfer classified these mechanisms into four categories.[6] The first group of mechanisms aims to offer a reward to the implementation actors, for example through a subsidy ('rewards'). The second group aims to punish recalcitrant actors to encourage them to act, for example through federal enforcement—which is, however, very rare ('sanctions'). The third group seeks to improve implementation by disseminating information about an obligation, for example through reports or action plans ('awareness-raising'). Finally, there are also rallying or co-ordination mechanisms, which encourage the cantons to implement international provisions in a certain way, such as inter-cantonal agreements or minimum harmonisation laws ('co-operation'). Such mechanisms seek a co-ordinated implementation of international obligations.

In the Swiss federal system, 'awareness-raising' mechanisms are the main (and sometimes the only) tools developed to encourage the implementation of human rights obligations at subnational level (Kaempfer, 2023). As far as engagement is concerned, we will see in the following sections that these mechanisms are merely invitations and have little power over subnational policy processes.

3.4 Ratification and Implementation of the Istanbul Convention

This section describes the ratification process of the Istanbul Convention and the 'domestic implementation mechanisms' that have been established to encourage subnational units to use and engage with the Convention.

3.4.1 Ratification of the Istanbul Convention

In preparation for the ratification of the Istanbul Convention, the consultation procedure took place between October 2015 and January 2016. The project sent into consultation by the Federal Office of Justice stated that 'globally, Swiss law fulfils the requirements of the Convention', but acknowledges that 'a few points must be clarified with regards to cantonal competences [...] notably on the question of whether there exist enough shelter possibilities for victims' (*our translation*).[7] All the cantons, the major political parties, and interested institutions and organisations were invited to submit their position. The vast

---

[6] A similar categorisation of policy instruments was made by Bemelmans-Videc, Rist and Vedung in their book 'Carrots, sticks, and sermons: Policy instruments and their evaluation' (Bemelmans-Videc et al., 1998).

[7] Office fédéral de la justice, « Projet mis en consultation: Convention du Conseil de l'Europe du 11 mai 2011 sur la prévention et la lutte contre la violence à l'égard des femmes et la violence domestique (convention d'Istanbul)», Berne, 2015, 2.

majority of the participants supported Switzerland's ratification. Three cantons (Luzern, Schwyz and Thurgau) and one party (the Swiss People's Party) opposed the ratification, along with a few institutions and organisations.[8]

Therefore, on 2 December 2016, the Federal Council requested the Swiss parliament approve the Istanbul Convention, which it did on 16 June 2017. The Federal Council then ratified the Convention on 14 December 2017, and the Convention entered into force for Switzerland on 1 April 2018.

This procedure shows how an explanatory report on ratification can orient the way cantonal authorities will use a treaty. By indicating that the Swiss legal order is already largely in line with the content of the treaty, the report sends the message to the relevant authorities that they will have almost no measures to take to comply with the Convention. As we will observe, this does not accurately reflect reality.

3.4.2 Designation of Implementing Bodies at the Federal and Cantonal Levels

With regard to implementation, Article 10 of the Istanbul Convention states that parties shall 'designate or establish one or more official bodies responsible for the co-ordination, implementation, monitoring and evaluation of policies and measures'.[9] The Explanatory report specifies that '[t]he term 'official body' is to be understood as any entity or institution within government'.[10] It adds that '[r]egarding the tasks of implementation, monitoring and evaluating this body should be in existence on the respective level of a Party's structure which is responsible for the carrying out of the measures. This means that in a federal government structure it may be necessary to have more than one body'.[11] Despite this, Switzerland decided to designate only one official body: the Domestic Violence Domain of the Federal Office for Gender Equality (BFEG).[12]

However, in the case of the Istanbul Convention, in addition to this single official body, Swiss federal authorities designated other specific organs to ensure the implementation of the Convention at the cantonal level, although they were not designated as official bodies. The Conference of Cantonal Ministers for Justice and Police and the Conference of Cantonal Ministers of Social Affairs mandated the Swiss Conference against Domestic Violence

---

[8] Conseil fédéral, «Message concernant l'approbation de la convention du Conseil de l'Europe sur la prévention et la lutte contre la violence à l'égard des femmes et la violence domestique», Berne, 2016, 169–170 (Message du Conseil fédéral). (These documents are also available in German).

[9] Council of Europe, 'Council of Europe Convention on preventing and combating violence against women and domestic violence,' Istanbul, 11 May 2011.

[10] *Explanatory Report* 13.

[11] Ibid.

[12] *Message du Conseil fédéral* 249.

(CSVD) to facilitate the inter-cantonal implementation of the Convention.[13] These so-called inter-cantonal conferences are recent instruments of federalism in Switzerland, which provide cantons with an arena for horizontal co-ordination and informal access to the national level (Vatter, 2018, p. 75). Different types of inter-cantonal conferences exist: the Conference of cantonal governments, the most important of these conferences, constitutes the first type. It was set up in 1993, 'to ensure that the cantonal interests are considered in the Europeanization process' (Vatter, 2018, p. 75). Second, there are twelve conferences of ministers, such as the Conference of Cantonal Ministers for Justice and Police and the Cantonal Ministers of Social Affairs. Third, there are inter-cantonal conferences of experts, which regroup specialised civil servants from the cantonal administrations, such as the CSVD.

The CSVD was founded in 2013, so that cantonal civil servants in charge of domestic violence could speak with one voice in cases of consultation procedures or other national projects regarding domestic violence. Before that, these civil servants were regrouped in two regional conferences. These two conferences—a Latin one (the *Conférence latine contre la violence domestique*) and a German one (the *Konferenz der Interventionsstellen, Projekte und Fachstellen gegen häusliche Gewalt der deutschen Schweiz*)—still often meet to exchange experience and collaborate on specific projects. An organisational difference between the two linguistic regions exists: in the Latin part, civil servants in charge of domestic violence work within the cantonal *Bureau de l'égalité* ('Office for Gender Equality'), while in the German part, they are usually attached to the Justice and Security cantonal department.[14]

The choice of the institutional anchorage of where the main responsibility for treaty implementation is placed is not a coincidence. By choosing either a gender equality office or a Justice and Security department, the subnational authorities participate in the framing of the implementation of the IC and place the emphasis on either the equality aspects of the treaty (including both prevention and fight against both violence against women and domestic violence) or a narrower emphasis on domestic violence. It is important to mention here that members of the CSVD—who are responsible for the policy combating domestic violence in their canton—are, for the French-speaking cantons, cantonal offices for gender equality, but for the German-speaking and Italian-speaking cantons, they are intervention centres and services against domestic violence in departments either of interior, of justice and police, or of social affairs, or in the cantonal police. In certain cantons, the implementation of the IC is thus mainly framed as an issue of domestic violence, while it is more broadly an issue of violence against women and of domestic violence, both linked to gender equality issues in other cantons.

---

[13] BFEG, «Concept de mise en œuvre», Berne, 2018, 15.

[14] Interview with the Head of the Office for Family Policy and Gender Equality, Neuchâtel, 13 March 2020.

3.4.3 Role of the BFEG in Subnational Implementation

Upon receiving its mandate, the CSVD published a report on the implementation of the Istanbul Convention at the cantonal level,[15] which took stock of relevant measures taken by cantons and identified seven priority fields for the first phase of the implementation. Shortly after the publication of this report, on 29 October 2018, the BFEG issued an 'Implementation Concept', which aims to clarify the collaboration between the federal state and the cantons. This document acknowledges the fact that large parts of the Convention fall into the competences of the cantons and specifies that in such cases, the cantons are responsible for completing the necessary measures.[16] Accordingly, the Conference of Cantonal Ministers for Justice and Police and the Conference of Cantonal Ministers of Social Affairs agreed to prioritise six fields during the first phase of the Convention's implementation,[17] which lasted from mid-2018 to the first Swiss State Report to the Council of Europe (see Article 68 of the Convention), initially due in 2020, but which was finally submitted in June 2021.

In 2022, the federal government (after the request of the federal parliament) charged the BFEG to draft a national action plan 2022–2026 for the implementation of the Istanbul Convention.[18] This action plan identifies priority fields and measures to be taken during this period, both at the federal and cantonal levels. Most of the measures regard information campaigns to the public and training for professional staff and volunteers, for which funding was made available. The BFEG also co-ordinates the implementation and the monitoring of this action plan.

This national action plan, as well as the report and implementation concept mentioned in this section, serve an informational purpose towards the cantons, informing them of where their efforts should focus with regard to the implementation of the Convention.

3.4.4 Role of the CSVD as a Link Between the BFEG and the Cantons

As the BFEG does not have contact with individual cantons, the CSVD acts as a 'seismograph on the field'[19] for them. The BFEG has regular exchanges with

---

[15] CSVD, «Mise en œuvre de la Convention d'Istanbul au niveau des cantons: Etat des lieux et mesures à entreprendre – rapport de la Conférence Suisse contre la Violence Domestique», Berne, 2018, p. 3.

[16] BFEG, «Concept de mise en œuvre», Berne, 2018, p. 11. This document was written in co-operation with the Conference of Cantonal Ministers for Justice and Police and the Conference of Cantonal Ministers of Social Affairs.

[17] One of the seven priority fields regarded was education. It was therefore transferred to the Conference of Cantonal Ministers of Education.

[18] Conseil fédéral, «Plan d'action national de la Suisse en vue de la mise en œuvre de la Convention d'Istanbul de 2022 à 2026», Berne, June 2022.

[19] Interview with the Deputy Director of the Federal Office for Gender Equality and one Member of the Federal Office of Justice, Berne, July 2020.

the CSVD; they meet once a year to discuss both sides' priorities. They sometimes also have common projects that the BFEG can financially support. Since the entry into force of the Istanbul Convention, the Conference of Cantonal Ministers for Justice and Police exchanges more regularly with the CSVD, as they often need advice from the technical experts.[20] In short, the CSVD works as a link between the cantons on the one hand, and the BFEG, the Conference of Cantonal Ministers for Justice and Police and the Cantonal Ministers of Social Affairs on the other.

Members of the CSVD meet three to four times a year. Interviewees stated that these meetings are primarily a place to exchange information and share experiences (notably what works well and what does not), to discuss potential common projects. Some CSVD members who are less familiar with the Istanbul Convention take advantage of the CSVD to ask fellow members which actions they should take to respond to the Convention. This is more likely to happen to members of smaller cantons, who have less resources.[21]

Furthermore, the CSVD creates working groups on specific topics, for prevention campaigns, or when they want to take a stance on a distinct political issue. These working groups serve as fora for officials to receive input from members of private associations active in relevant fields, such as shelter institutions.

Despite the foundation of the nationwide CSVD in 2013, the two regional conferences (Latin and German), remain active and seem to carry more importance than the CSVD. According to one CSVD member, the Latin conference meets at least five times per year and is able to produce more output, while CSVD meetings are limited to information exchange. This is probably because the regional conference existed before the CSVD and their members are less numerous, speak the same language, and, as a result, probably know each other better. Regional conferences, for instance, allow the creation of prevention campaigns and exhibitions. Cantons join forces to produce regional strategies.

With regard to the implementation of the Istanbul Convention, an important contribution of the CSVD is the 2018 report on the implementation at the cantonal level, which identified the seven priority fields. This report was written by the Committee of the CSVD—i.e. by the two co-presidents and two other members—in consultation with the CSVD as a whole.[22] The co-president of the CSVD explained how this report was produced: by translating and adapting the Istanbul Convention into priority fields of action through a back-and-forth process between the needs identified in the field and the content of the Convention. The report was drafted on this basis and was

---

[20] Interview with the Head of the Domestic Violence Co-ordination Office, St. Gallen, 19 January 2021, who is also one of the current co-presidents of the CSVD (there are always two co-presidents: one from the German region and one from the Latin region).

[21] Interview with the Head of the Domestic Violence Co-ordination Office, St. Gallen and Co-President of the CSVD (Zoom, 19 January 2021).

[22] Interview with the Head of the Office for the Promotion of Gender Equality and the Prevention of Violence (Geneva, 1 July 2020).

consequently produced exclusively at the cantonal level. Neither the BFEG, nor any other federal entity was consulted.

Overall, CSVD members see the CSVD as an implementation mechanism in the sense that it fosters the exchange of information and may serve for co-ordinating activities, thus contributing to the implementation of the Istanbul Convention. Ultimately, individual members are free to take or suggest implementing measures in their own canton. Moreover, we observe an institutionalised implementation process, with the designation of an 'official body' at the national level (the BFEG), and another state entity (the CSVD) mandated to facilitate implementation of the Convention at the inter-cantonal level (although not designated as an 'official body' as per art. 10 of the Convention). We also observe that the CSVD did not only act as a top-down implementing actor, but it also identifies the needs in the field in relation to the content of the Convention in a bottom-up manner, which overall, forms a back-and-forth process.

3.5 Ratification and Implementation of the Convention on the Rights of Persons with Disabilities

This section describes the ratification process of the Convention on the Rights of Persons with Disabilities and the 'domestic implementation mechanisms' that have been developed to encourage subnational units to use—and engage with—the Convention.

3.5.1 Ratification of the CRPD

In preparation for the ratification of the CRPD,[23] the consultation procedure took place between December 2010 and April 2011.[24] In a similar way to the consultation on the Istanbul Convention, the project states that 'the Swiss legal order complies in principle with the Convention, even if there are areas in which legislative adaptations might be necessary in order to take into account the specific requirements of the Convention as a whole' (*our translation*).[25] We will see that this statement, as for the case discussed above, does not accurately reflect reality. All the cantons, the major political parties, and interested institutions and organisations submitted their position. Most cantons expressly approved ratification or at least supported its principle.[26]

---

[23] Convention on the Rights of Persons with Disabilities (CRPD), RS 0.109.

[24] Conseil fédéral, Message portant approbation de la Convention du 13 décembre 2006 relative aux droits des personnes handicapées, Berne, 2012 (Message du Conseil fédéral CDPH), 608–609.

[25] Département fédéral des affaires étrangères, «Projet de rapport explicatif: Convention du 13 décembre 2006 relative aux droits des personnes handicapées», Berne, 2010, 7.

[26] Ibid.

However, four cantons (Appenzell Innerrhoden, Nidwald, Thurgau and Vaud) considered ratification superfluous due to sufficient legislation in this area.[27]

On 19 December 2012, the Federal Council requested the Swiss parliament approve the CRPD, which it did on 13 December 2013. The Federal Council then ratified the Convention on 15 April 2014, which entered into force for Switzerland on 15 May 2014.

As for the Istanbul Convention, the ratification procedure described above shows that an explanatory report on ratification already orients the uses of the treaty by the relevant subnational authorities. In the present case, the report implies that Swiss law is already largely in line with the Convention and therefore that subnational authorities do not need to act, or at least not much.

3.5.2 *Absence of a General Implementation Strategy*

In contrast with the implementation of the Istanbul Convention, neither the Federal Office for the Equality of Persons with Disabilities (BFEH) nor the Conference of Cantonal Delegates for Disability Issues adopted any implementation strategy for the CRPD. According to one of our interviewees, the Federal Council assumed that it would be enough to wait for spontaneous cantonal (and federal) legislative revisions and the implementation of the Convention would follow automatically.[28] Yet, Article 33 of the Convention, similar to article 10 of the Istanbul Convention, mandates the establishment of focal points responsible for implementing the Convention's provisions. In its Message on the Convention, the Federal Council considered that the BFEH would take on some of the duties of a federal 'focal point'.[29] For cantons, the Federal Council suggested that having focal points was desirable but not essential for the national application of the Convention.[30]

Switzerland has recently been criticised by the UN Committee on the Rights of Persons with Disabilities for the lack of a comprehensive strategy to implement the CRPD.[31] Therefore, the Committee recommended that Switzerland adopts 'a comprehensive disability strategy and action plan for implementing all Convention rights at all levels of government, and strengthen co-ordination and co-operation among entities at the federal, cantonal and

---

[27] Ibid.

[28] Interview with the Head of the BFEH, Berne, 10 May 2022.

[29] Message du Conseil fédéral CDPH, 653.

[30] Ibid.

[31] Committee on the Rights of Persons with Disabilities, Concluding observations on the initial report of Switzerland, CRPD/C/CHE/CO/1, para. 7.

municipal levels'.[32] In March 2023, the Federal Council adopted a new 'disability policy 2023–2026'.[33] The document fixes four priority fields of action (work, housing, benefits and participation). In terms of implementation, the report foresees the creation of committees in the four priority action fields to enhance the involvement and co-operation of the main actors.

Perhaps as a response to the federal government's slow progress in this area, at least two different groups of experts developed 'domestic implementation mechanisms' to encourage subnational units to engage with the treaty. These mechanisms are described below.

3.5.3 Creation of an Implementation Guide

At the University of Basel, a group of academic experts first gave specific input on the creation of several cantonal laws related to equality for persons with disabilities and secondly, created an implementation guide for the CRPD. These initiatives were not prompted by the Confederation but were instead driven by the voluntary efforts of certain cantons to implement the Convention.[34] Depending on the canton and the situation, the experts supported the cantons through an analysis of the existing legislation, interviews with members of the cantonal administration and the drafting of a first draft of the law (Schefer et al., 2022, p. 156ss). Our analysis shows that the guidance provided by the team of experts was instrumental in spurring not only the engagement of the cantonal legislators but also the translation of the Convention into numerous concrete measures. In a cross-cutting area such as the rights of persons with disabilities, one cannot expect every employee of the cantonal administration to be aware of all the international obligations that concern him or her.[35] The University's external perspective made it possible to support the legislative project against the scepticism or resistance of certain cantonal departments, and to bring an academic expertise where cantonal bureaucracies face uncertainties about how to interpret the CRPD, their obligations, as well as what they must and can do to implement the CRPD.[36] According to the editors of the implementation guide, the involvement of external experts also avoided an accumulation of roles by the department in charge, which was then perceived as credible and sufficiently removed from local politics (Schefer et al., 2022, p. 156).

The processes described above work by providing specific and targeted advice to parliamentarians in specific cantons. While such a mechanism may

---

[32] Ibid., para. 8.

[33] Bureau fédéral de l'égalité pour les personnes handicapées BFEH, «Politique du handicap 2023–2026», Berne, 10 March 2023.

[34] Interview with the Head of the BFEH, Berne, 10 May 2022.

[35] Interview with one of the experts involved in these policy processes, on Zoom, 6 October 2020.

[36] Ibid.

spur engagement with the obligations under the CRPD, it requires significant personal and budgetary resources. It is therefore hardly conceivable that it could be generalised to all cantons. However, based on positive experiences in some cantons, and with financial support from the Federal Office for the Equality of Persons with Disabilities (BFEH), the team of experts developed a guide to assist other cantons in engaging with the CRPD (Schefer et al., 2022). For the drafting of the guide, the experts met with persons with disabilities, the federal administration, the Conference of Cantonal Directors of Social Affairs and various organisations for the protection of persons with disabilities.[37] These interviews showed a significant disparity between the cantons in terms of their willingness to adopt provisions to implement the CRPD.[38] Their respective interest in the guide was also very different. While some cantons claimed that they had already met their obligations under the Convention, others recognised that their legislation was insufficient and were eager to use the guide.[39]

The guide is structured to facilitate the work of the relevant cantonal authorities. It contains four parts. The first part outlines the international and federal obligations of the cantons in the field of equality for persons with disabilities and identifies the need for action in cantonal legislation. The second part formulates some suggestions as to how cantonal legislation in this field could be structured. The third part contains a model law with some explanations. Finally, the fourth part takes the form of a commentary on the CRPD specifically for the cantons.

This example illustrates how, in the absence of a strategy adopted by federal or inter-cantonal authorities, experts have taken the lead to meet the needs expressed by certain cantons. The guide is a 'domestic implementation mechanism' that emerged from 'below' in a 'bottom-up' manner while taking a top-down legal perspective (creating a model law to be taken and adapted by cantons).

3.5.4 *Dissemination of 'Good Practice' on a Website*

In the absence of a federal implementation strategy, the Swiss Centre of Expertise in Human Rights[40] created another 'domestic implementation mechanism' to encourage subnational units to engage with the CRPD. This

---

[37] Ibid.

[38] Ibid.

[39] Ibid.

[40] The Swiss Centre of Expertise in Human Rights was a pilot project set up in 2011 on behalf of the Federal Government. It was set up as a university network and its services included reports, advanced training, legal or social science studies, databases, websites, information material, conferences, and other events, as well as experts' participation at panel discussions (Swiss Centre of Expertise in Human Rights, About the SCHR). The SCHR is no longer active and has been replaced with a National Human Rights Institute in spring 2023.

mechanism operates through a dedicated website (www.cdph-exemplespratiques.ch). The website disseminates information and highlights examples of good practices from various Swiss cantons to implement the CRPD, with the goal of making the Convention known to the public and encouraging engagement by subnational actors.[41] By presenting examples of good practices from cantons, the website also gives credit and recognition. The mechanism functions through a back-and-forth process, taking information from some cantons and making it available to all.

3.6 DISCUSSION

3.6.1 *Around the Ratification of Treaties: A First Phase to Orient the Engagement of Cantonal Political Authorities*

The ratification procedures of our two case studies are quite alike. In both instances, the Federal Council (government) considered, during the pre-parliamentary consultation phase, that the Swiss legal system was already in compliance with most of the treaty's obligations. Such a statement, from the country's highest executive authority, decisively orients the way in which the subnational authorities will use and engage (or not) with the treaty. As discussed in subsequent chapters, subnational entities often need guidance to effectively engage with international treaties. As such, orientation from the federal level is of utmost importance. In our case studies, the Federal Council seems to have at times underestimated or downplayed the effort needed from subnational units to implement the treaty.

3.6.2 *Varieties of International Treaties Implementation Strategies: Top-Down or Bottom-Up?*

This chapter shows that no formal institutional procedure exists to guarantee the implementation of international human rights treaties at the subnational level in Switzerland. However, we observe that both the Istanbul Convention and the CRPD require the designation of state entities (at the national and sometimes at the subnational level) responsible for implementation. While these actors designed an implementation strategy for the Istanbul Convention, none of them did so for the CRPD (so far, but the "Disability Policy 2023–2026" makes a step in this direction). Moreover, in the first case, we observe that federal authorities are increasingly active in creating implementation dynamics, including most recently a federal action plan launched by the Federal Council to implement the Istanbul Convention at the different levels of the Confederation (national, cantonal and communal).[42] In the case of the

---

[41] Interview with a scientific collaborator who worked on the project, 6 October 2020.

[42] Conseil fédéral, «Plan d'action national de la Suisse en vue de la mise en œuvre de la Convention d'Istanbul de 2022 à 2026», Berne, June 2022.

CRPD, we did not observe such an implementation dynamic from the federal level. This may have been one reason why academic experts stepped up to take the lead, creating a comprehensive implementation guide and a website to encourage cantons to reform the relevant policies. By providing an accessible repository of information, these efforts aim to make it easier for cantons to engage with the treaties. The mechanisms developed by different experts should indeed help them identify and address the necessary changes.

We also demonstrated that these implementation mechanisms are never purely top-down. In the case of the CRPD, the fact that the guide came into existence and can now be used in a top-down way is due to reasons originating bottom-up: the positive experiences observed in certain cantons inspired academic experts to devise tools to address the lack of resources provided at the federal or inter-cantonal level. For the Istanbul Convention, while the implementation process may at first sight appear as a top-down process, we observe that it is an iterative process (as observed in other studies: Donald & Speck, 2020; Haglund & Stryker, 2015; Risse et al., 1999), with the CSVD going back and forth between the needs in the field and the content of the Convention.

3.6.3 *Mechanisms at Stake in the Two Case Studies*

Domestic implementation mechanisms for international treaty obligations in Switzerland can take various forms: sanctions, rewards, awareness-raising and co-operation (Kaempfer, 2023). In our two case studies, the mechanisms involved were essentially awareness-raising (such mechanisms are sometimes called sermons in the literature (Bemelmans-Videc et al., 1998)). These information mechanisms include the experts' implementation guide and the website for the CRPD provided by the Swiss Centre of Expertise in Human Rights, as well as the BFEG's implementation concept and national action plan, and the CSVD's implementation report for the Istanbul Convention. Such mechanisms are rather 'soft': they seek to change the behaviour of the cantonal authorities through information and advice, but such 'awareness-raising' mechanisms do not sanction cantons for implementation failures, nor do they imply financial incentives or a strong involvement of the federal level in achieving a co-ordinated implementation at the subnational level. 'Awareness-raising' mechanisms may come with reputational gains or risks ('naming and shaming') and they can contribute to changing the political will in the areas in question; however, they usually do not allow for a systematic implementation of international law.

Constance Kaempfer examined the various mechanisms used in Switzerland to implement human rights treaty obligations on the one hand and obligations from bilateral treaties between Switzerland and the European Union on the other hand. She found that information-based mechanisms are, by far, the most commonly used in the field of human rights obligations, while the Confederation shows a greater willingness to employ other, including 'harder' mechanisms such as sanctions and rewards in the field of European Union Law (Kaempfer, 2023). Indeed, despite the existence of 'awareness-raising' mechanisms, the international conventions studied have not been systematically implemented in all cantons, as the following chapters will demonstrate, and as other studies have similarly found (Belser & Egli, 2022). In its concluding observations on the initial report of Switzerland on the CRPD,[43] the Committee on the Rights of Persons with Disabilities noted with concern the lack of measures taken on almost all the specific rights guaranteed by the Convention. Similarly, the GREVIO's baseline evaluation report on the implementation of the Istanbul Convention in Switzerland highlighted 'considerable disparities between cantons' approaches, policies, legislation and measures to combat violence against women. The failure to harmonise practices and services, and sometimes a lack of inter-cantonal co-operation, may lead to varying levels of protection for women victims of violence depending on where they live'.[44]

In summary, the existing mechanisms for implementing human rights treaties at the subnational level are limited. Simply multiplying the number of 'awareness-raising' mechanisms may not always be sufficient. Instead, a certain degree of harmonisation at the inter-cantonal or federal level may be necessary. For example, the establishment of rallying mechanisms could improve engagement with human rights treaties. To improve our understanding of the larger iterative process that may lead to engagement at the subnational level, the following chapters will examine the actual experiences of subnational actors (such as parliamentarians, bureaucrats and civil society) with international treaties. By gaining insight into their needs and perspectives, as well as the way they interact with human rights treaties, we want to understand the process of using such treaties and political authorities engaging with them.

3.7 Conclusion

This chapter has highlighted the ratification and implementation mechanisms of international human rights treaties in Switzerland's federalist settings. While the ratification of treaties follows a formal procedure, our two case studies show that there is no preconceived procedure with regard to implementation. Therefore, we observe that implementation processes follow very diverse patterns. Several state entities responsible for the implementation of the Istanbul Convention designed implementation strategies and even a federal action plan, in what could be characterised as a top-down process. For the CRPD, despite the establishment of a focal point responsible for implementation, we observe that there has been no implementation strategy at the federal or inter-cantonal level. Thus, academic experts produced alternative tools to lead the implementation process.

[43] CRPD/C/CHE/CO/1.
[44] GREVIO/Inf(2022)28, p. 74.

This chapter also showed that in our two case studies, the mechanisms involved to spur subnational engagement with the treaties are 'soft'. They are essentially information-based, i.e. 'awareness-raising' mechanisms, which seek to change the behaviour of the subnational authorities through information and advice. Other types of mechanisms, such as sanction or co-operation, were not used. Mechanisms of this kind have been successfully used to implement obligations in the field of bilateral agreements between Switzerland and the European Union (see, for example, (Kaempfer, 2023). It is conceivable that similar mechanisms could also be developed in the field of human rights. However, exploring this idea falls outside the scope of this book. Instead, in the upcoming chapters, we will delve deeper into the examination of individual cantons. We will investigate how local actors such as bureaucrats, elected officials and representatives of civil society—oftentimes as a result of these strategies and mechanisms—are using international treaties to further their own local objectives, agendas and strategies, thereby often contributing to their implementation.

References

Belser, E. M., & Egli, S. (2022). Les atouts du fédéralisme pour les droits humains. In Centre suisse de compétence pour les droits humains (CSDH) (Ed.), *Renforcer les droits humains en Suisse: Nouvelles idées pour la politique et la pratique* (pp. 41–58). buch&netz.

Bemelmans-Videc, M.-L., Rist, R. C., & Vedung, E. (1998). *Carrots, Sticks and Sermons: Policy Instruments and Their Evalutation*. Transaction Publishers.

Cassese, A. (2005). *International Law*. Oxford University Press.

Comstock, A. L. (2021). *Committed to Rights: UN Human Rights Treaties and Legal Paths for Commitment and Compliance*. Cambridge University Press.

De Beco, G. (2010). *Non-judicial Mechanisms for the Implementation of Human Rights in the European States*. Bruylant. http://books.google.com/books?id=uJxEAQAAIAAJ

Denza, E. (2018). The Relationship between International and National Law. In M. D. Evans (Ed.), *International Law* (pp. 383–411). Oxford University Press.

Donald, A., & Speck, A.-K. (2020). The Dynamics of Domestic Human Rights Implementation: Lessons from Qualitative Research in Europe. *Journal of Human Rights Practice, 12*(1), 48–70. https://doi.org/10.1093/jhuman/huaa007

Haglund, L., & Stryker, R. (2015). *Closing the Rights Gap: From Human Rights to Social Transformation*. University of California Press.

Jensen, S. L. B., Lagoutte, S., & Lorion, S. (2019). The Domestic Institutionalisation of Human Rights: An Introduction. *Nordic Journal of Human Rights, 37*(3), 165–176.

Kaempfer, C. (2021). Domestic Mechanisms for the Implementation of International Obligations in the Swiss Cantons. *Swiss Review of International and European Law, 31*(4), 541–563.

Kaempfer, C. (2023). *Les mécanismes de mise en oeuvre du droit international par les cantons suisses: études de cas dans les domaines des droits humains et des accords bilatéraux Suisse-UE*. Sui generis.

Murray, R. (2020). Addressing the Implementation Crisis: Securing Reparation and Righting Wrongs. *Journal of Human Rights Practice, 12*(1), 1–21.

Murray, R., & De Vos, C. (2020). Behind the State: Domestic Mechanisms and Procedures for the Implementation of Human Rights Judgments and Decisions. *Journal of Human Rights Practice, 12*(1), 22–47.

Nuspliger, K. (2006). La participation des parlements cantonaux au processus décisionnel en politique européenne. In Conférence des gouvernements cantonaux (Ed.), *Entre adhésion à l'UE et voie bilatérale: réflexions et besoin de réformes du point de vue des cantons* (pp. 76). Schulthess.

Risse, T., Risse-Kappen, T., Ropp, S. C., & Sikkink, K. (1999). *The Power of Human Rights: International Norms and Domestic Change* (Vol. 66). Cambridge University Press.

Schefer, M., Martin, C., & Hess-Klein, C. (2022). *Leitfaden für eine behindertenrechtliche Gesetzgebung in den Kantonen*. Weblaw.

Simmons, B. (2012). *Mobilizing for Human Rights: International Law in Domestic Politics*. Cambridge University Press.

Vatter, A. (2018). *Swiss Federalism: The Transformation of a Federal Model*. Routledge.

Open Access This chapter is licensed under the terms of the Creative Commons Attribution 4.0 International License (http://creativecommons.org/licenses/by/4.0/), which permits use, sharing, adaptation, distribution and reproduction in any medium or format, as long as you give appropriate credit to the original author(s) and the source, provide a link to the Creative Commons license and indicate if changes were made.

The images or other third party material in this chapter are included in the chapter's Creative Commons license, unless indicated otherwise in a credit line to the material. If material is not included in the chapter's Creative Commons license and your intended use is not permitted by statutory regulation or exceeds the permitted use, you will need to obtain permission directly from the copyright holder.

CHAPTER 4

Varieties of How Actors Use Human Rights Treaties in Subnational Policy Processes

Abstract In this chapter, we examine the varieties of how actors *use* international human rights treaties in policy processes at the subnational level. As explained in Chapters 1 and 2, our case studies are the Istanbul Convention (IC) and the Convention on the Rights of Persons with Disabilities (CRPD) in Swiss cantons. Here, we identify the most relevant actors and how they come to know about a treaty, and we then categorise various uses according to the actors and to the stage of the policy process in which the actors intervene. We find that various subnational actors—including bureaucrats, elected politicians (members of cantonal parliaments or governments), civil society representatives and academic experts—use treaties according to their own local interests, agendas and strategies. The uses of the treaties often occur along a continuous and incremental process involving back and forth and both top-down and bottom-up dynamics. In the policy process, subnational actors use treaties to (a) set issues on the policy agenda and (b) to support claims (new ones or existing ones). If the relevant subnational political authorities use a treaty with a view to further its implementation, we qualify this type of use as an engagement, which we will address in Chapter 5.

Keywords CRPD · Implementation Policy Processes · Istanbul Convention · Switzerland · Specialised Bureaucrats · Uses of human rights treaties

4.1 INTRODUCTION

In Switzerland, both the Istanbul Convention (IC) and the Convention on the Rights of Persons with Disabilities (CRPD) concern, to a large extent, cantonal competences such as education, police, construction, social system and health. As Chapter 3 has shown, there is no formal, nor automatic procedure through which subnational units are compelled to engage with these international treaties and the obligations therein. Although Switzerland can incur international state responsibility if subnational units fail to implement obligations within their competences, there is no pre-set federal strategy to coerce or command subnational units to engage with these two treaties. In practice, federal surveillance (art. 49 para. 2 of the Swiss Federal Constitution) is limited as it involves encroaches on cantonal competences (Kaempfer, 2023).

We argue that it is necessary to study the subnational uses of a treaty, to understand how political authorities (i.e. parliament and government) eventually engage with human rights treaties (Chapter 5). As mentioned in the introduction (Chapter 1), a use of a treaty is an instance in which an actor strategically or instrumentally refers to a treaty and works with it, e.g. by citing it or by relying on it in a parliamentary speech, a draft law, a report or a discussion, etc. Studying the uses of a treaty allows us to capture what subnational actors involved in policy processes *do* with treaties, and eventually sheds light on how human rights law works in practice in subnational policy processes. So, this chapter aims to answer the following question: how do actors use international human rights treaties in subnational policy processes?

We analyse the varieties of *actors* who use the Istanbul Convention and the CRPD in cantonal policy processes—that we consider as international law intermediaries (Miaz et al., 2024; Pélisse, 2019; Talesh & Pélisse, 2019)—as well as the variety of *uses* (Merry, 2006). Section 4.1.1 first highlights who the key subnational actors are and how they come to know about the existence of a treaty. Then, in Sects. 4.2 and 4.3, we present the different types of uses by subnational actors. In Sect. 4.2, we show how different actors use the treaties to set a specific issue on the cantonal political agenda. Section 4.3 shows how actors use treaties as legal and political arguments to support their (new or existing) claims and approaches. As explained in Chapter 1, sometimes the use of a treaty by a subnational actor triggers the engagement of the relevant subnational political authorities with the treaty and those subnational authorities begin to study the treaty and to formulate and adopt policy measures. These 'success stories' are part of Chapter 5 where we examine the patterns of engagement by political authorities. Here in Chapter 4, we only present the early uses sometimes leading up to later engagements.

Treaties provide opportunities. A priori, subnational actors could perceive treaties as obligations and constraints. However, our results show that cantonal specialised policy bureaucrats often perceive them as a political opportunity, a legitimation tool and a resource.

We also observe that the use of human rights treaties in cantonal policy processes is not systematic, nor linear. Instead, specialised policy bureaucrats, members of cantonal parliaments, and other actors involved in subnational policymaking processes use human rights treaties in various ways which depend on both their strategic goals and on the local political context. As a result, the use of international norms is patchy, complex and very uneven. What is more, the various types of uses of international law identified at different stages in the policy process may interact together, often via a self-reinforcing process.

4.1.1 Who Are the Key Actors Who Use Human Rights Treaties in Subnational Policy Processes and How Do They Come to Know About a Treaty?

Before presenting the varieties of how subnational actors use international human rights treaties, we briefly present who the key actors are and how they come to know the existence of a human rights treaty.

The first group of key actors are 'specialised policy bureaucrats'. We refer here to the notion of 'policy bureaucrat', discussed by Page and Jenkins (Page & Jenkins, 2005). In their analysis, these authors emphasised that policymaking is not exclusively a political activity but also a bureaucratic one. They argued that the processes within policy bureaucracies are more than just subordinate acts and that officials have a certain degree of discretion in making policy decisions. This includes the ability to design 'the legal, financial, and organizational arrangements which go to make the policy' (Page, 2012). However, these proposals usually require approval from their superiors, ministers, government members or parliament. Consequently, bureaucrats must anticipate their reactions and develop proposals that are likely to gain their approval. In this book, specialised policy bureaucrats are bureaucrats specialising in a particular policy field (gender equality, domestic violence, disability policy) and who can be, because of this position, specifically committed to a particular cause (gender equality, women's rights, disability rights, human rights). As we will show, these actors often use international human rights treaties.

The specialised bureaucrats we interviewed underline that, in their specific domain (violence against women, domestic violence, disability) the treaties are 'omnipresent', they are 'everywhere'. Information about the existence and ratification of a human rights treaty is communicated by the federal offices—the Federal Office for Gender Equality and the Federal Office of Equality for Persons with Disabilities—and in the inter-cantonal conferences, such as the Swiss Conference on Domestic Violence or the Conference of Cantonal Delegates for Disability Issues. In these information exchanges, concrete topics in relation to the implementation of the treaty are discussed with colleagues from other cantons. An interviewee mentions, for example, how events organised by the Federal Office for Gender Equality helped to inform specialised policy bureaucrats of the existence of a treaty that needs to be implemented:

I was at a conference [...] where the Istanbul Convention was presented and also the expectations were communicated relatively clearly, what is expected of the cantons. And for me, that was already such an 'aha effect', where I really heard for the first time what is in store for us, what the experiences are – not least also that other cantons are much further along here. And that really fired us up and motivated us, drove us to really move forward quickly.[1]

Conferences, meetings and working groups organised by federal authorities or inter-cantonal instances can encourage cantonal bureaucrats to use a treaty. Law reforms and policy changes taking place in other cantons also encourage them to use a treaty. The reviewing process through which the UN Committee on the Rights of Persons with Disabilities or the Group of Experts on Action against Violence against Women and Domestic Violence (GREVIO) monitor the implementation of the treaty also participates in the information of specialised policy bureaucrats, sometimes after the recommendations are communicated by these bodies. Finally, these specialised policy bureaucrats are in contact with the 'field', including civil society organisations (CSOs), frontline workers and institutions working 'on the ground', and people directly concerned by the issues on which the treaties focus (i.e. people with disabilities, those affected by gender stereotypes or domestic violence). To one of the interviewees, the CRPD has become unavoidable: this was one of the first documents he read when he started working in this domain, 'because it is there, it is present, it is everywhere. It permeates us a little bit from all sides. As I said, it is a driving force, a groundswell that is taking everything in its path'.[2]

We will see that subnational cantonal members of parliament (MPs) also use international treaties but often only after other subnational actors draw the MPs attention to a treaty. Cantonal MPs are seldom specialists in domestic violence, disability or human rights (only some of them are), and they often come to know of international treaties through other actors. The following provides a useful illustration of the key role of actors outside the subnational parliament to inform cantonal MPs about the existence of a human rights treaty: in the case of the Istanbul Convention, the Women's Group of the Swiss Social Democratic Party received in 2018 a representative of the NGO *Brava* (which is part of the NGO network *Netzwerk Istanbul Konvention*, a coalition of NGOs created in order to observe the implementation of the treaty) in order to get to know the Istanbul Convention. Following this meeting, the Women's Group of the Social Democratic Party drafted a parliamentary interpellation, together with this NGO. The interpellation was addressed to cantonal MPs of the Social Democratic Party, with a request that

---

[1] Interview with a Head of Service, Social Security Office, Schaffhausen, 19 May 2021.
[2] Interview with a Head of Domain, Social Action Department, Jura, 6 April 2022.

they submit it to their respective government.³ The authors asked questions related to the implementation of the Istanbul Convention, with the aim to 'map' existing measures in all cantons. This interpellation was submitted, at times with modifications, in several cantons. This example shows that cantonal MPs are likely to get to know international treaties through the mediation of other subnational actors, notably civil society organisations. The example also shows that cantonal MPs who are specifically committed to a specific cause, like gender equality and women's rights, or disability rights, are interested and likely to be aware that a treaty exists and can use the treaty to advance their cause.

Once a subnational actor has found out about the existence of a human rights treaty, how exactly can subnational actors use the treaty? We identified two main varieties of uses: agenda-setting (Sect. 4.2) and supporting claims and policy approaches (Sect. 4.3)—claims on specific treaty obligations, claims to support demands from 'the ground' and claims to support existing policy approaches.

4.2 Using Treaties for Agenda-Setting

In this section, we show that subnational actors use international treaties as a means to set a public problem on the cantonal political agenda. Treaty ratifications create a 'policy window' (Kingdon, 2014) for bureaucratic, parliamentary, and civil society actors who defend equality's and the women's cause (Bereni, 2021; Bereni & Revillard, 2018; Childs & Krook, 2009), disability rights (Heyer, 2015; Revillard, 2019; Vanhala, 2011), or more generally human rights. We will first focus on specialised policy bureaucrats as agenda-setters (subsection 4.2.1). We will then show how a variety of other subnational actors such as members of cantonal parliaments, civil society actors and experts, also use treaties to put their implementation on the political agenda (subsection 4.2.2).

4.2.1 Specialised Policy Bureaucrats as Agenda-Setters

Specialised policy bureaucrats may use international human rights treaties as an opportunity to put an issue on the political agenda in their canton. For example, with respect to the Istanbul Convention, the Head of the Office for Family Policy and Gender Equality (the 'Equality Delegate') succeeded in initiating a law-making process in 2018 in the canton of Neuchâtel (173,333 inhabitants in 2021)—around the same time as the entry into force of the IC. The initiative led to the adoption of a new law on combatting domestic violence. The Equality Delegate contributed to the elaboration of the new

---

³ Interview with a member of the cantonal parliament (*Social Democratic Party*), Neuchâtel, 5 June 2020.

law, replacing a former one on the fight against violence in couple relationships, 'to adapt it to the Istanbul Convention'.[4] Thus, the IC provided the motivation and set the timing for launching a legislative reform: the Equality Delegate used the ratification of the treaty and the obligation to implement it as a means to support her draft legislation. The report presenting the new legislation to the cantonal parliament mentioned that the canton 'will be able to honour its obligations coming from the signature of the Istanbul Convention'.[5] In this example, the Equality Delegate used the treaty as a tool to set the issue of domestic violence on the political agenda, and to push for a law-making process involving the cantonal parliament. The Istanbul Convention was also used as a cognitive resource in the formulation of the new law and to reframe the public problem of violence in 'couple relationships' into a more global public problem of 'domestic violence', while emphasising the fact that such violence is gender-based violence. The next chapter, Chapter 5, will delve into how this use of the treaty resulted in an engagement with the Istanbul Convention.

In several other cantons, specialised policy bureaucrats also used the Istanbul Convention for agenda-setting. Specialised bureaucrats launched a policy process to engage with the Istanbul Convention either through a law reform, through an action plan or by asking for means to implement the IC. The role of bureaucrats setting the issue of the implementation of the Istanbul Convention on the agenda is also observed in the case of the CRPD, but less frequently. In Valais (346,562 inhabitants in 2021), the Head of the co-ordination office for questions in the field of disability explained that the former law did not include a part on the rights of persons with disabilities.

> In order to have a law that also corresponds to the request of the UN, we contacted [a Professor] and his team and we asked them to make a partial revision of our law to integrate this into our law. And then they made a proposal with comments.[6]

In collaboration with the academic experts and based on recommendations collected during meetings with people with disabilities, specialised bureaucrats prepared a revision of the cantonal law on the rights and inclusion of people with disabilities and thus succeeded in creating an engagement by the subnational political authorities (see Chapter 5).

Thus, specialised policy bureaucrats—as they are responsible for the main field addressed by the treaties, and the treaties provide them with an opportunity to advance their expertise—act as agenda-setters (Guaschino, 2023).

---

[4] Interview with the Head of the Cantonal Office for Family Policy and Equality, Neuchâtel, 13 March 2020.

[5] Cantonal government of Neuchâtel, « *Rapport du Conseil d'État au Grand Conseil à l'appui d'un projet de loi sur la lutte contre la violence domestique* » 2019, p. 24.

[6] Interview with the Head of the Co-ordinating Office for Disability Issues, Social Action Department, Valais, 23 March 2022.

To these specialised policy bureaucrats, treaties are useful 'because when we have to put together a file for parliament, the [treaty] allows us to rely on it because it is a strong lever that is recognised by all'.[7] Thus, to them, the treaties provide opportunities and resources—international law offering a strong argument of authority—to reform and extend a policy program.

4.2.2 Members of Cantonal Parliaments and Civil Society Actors as Agenda-Setters

Specialised policy bureaucrats are not the only ones who use treaties to set an issue on the political agenda. Cantonal MPs, civil society actors and experts (such as academic actors) use treaties for agenda-setting. Let us first turn to cantonal MPs. Cantonal MPs use parliamentary interventions, such as questions,[8] interpellations,[9] postulates,[10] and motions,[11] to put the implementation of the treaties, or issues related to them, on the political agenda. In the case of the Istanbul Convention, cantonal parliament members who are committed to the causes of equality—mainly members of the Social Democratic Party, the Greens or other left-wing parties[12]—used the treaty to request information on its implementation, or to put a specific issue or obligation on the political agenda. In the case of the CRPD, some members of cantonal parliaments who are committed to the defence of disability rights used parliamentary interventions to request a new comprehensive law on inclusion and the rights of persons with disabilities or to ask for measures on specific issues related to the treaty. While most of the elected politicians who use the CRPD are from the above-mentioned left-wing parties, some individual politicians affiliated with other parties also used the treaties for agenda-setting. Some of these politicians are committed in civil society organisations (CSOs) of persons with disabilities and their families or in disability rights movements, and some of them live with disabilities.

A typical way to put the implementation of a convention on the cantonal political agenda is to request information on it through a parliamentary question or interpellation. In the case of the Istanbul Convention, we explained

---

[7] Interview with a Head of Domain, Social Action Department, Jura, 6 April 2022.

[8] A question is a written request for information to the cantonal government on current issues concerning the canton.

[9] An interpellation is a request for a reasoned explanation, addressed in writing to the cantonal government and concerning any matter affecting the canton and falling within its competence.

[10] A postulate is a proposal from the cantonal parliament to the cantonal government to study the advisability of taking a measure or legislating in a particular area and to draw up a report on the results of its study, with proposals if necessary.

[11] A motion is an order from the cantonal parliament to the cantonal government to study a question, take a measure or present a report.

[12] *Christian Social Party* (Jura), *«Ensemble à gauche» Party* (Geneva), and *Alternative Left Party* (Zurich).

above that the Women's Group of the Social Democratic Party drafted an intervention template with the support of an NGO, which was sent out to all the cantonal sections of the Social Democratic Party, with a suggestion to submit it to their respective governments.[13] As a consequence, several cantonal MPs of the Social Democratic Party submitted these interventions, setting the political agenda of their own parliament. For instance, in Neuchâtel the interpellation 'Istanbul Convention: what about its implementation?'[14] was filed by a cantonal MP of the Social Democratic Party on 11 November 2018. In Schwyz, the interpellation 'Violence against women – what does Canton Schwyz?'[15] was filed on 5 December 2018 by two MPs of the Social Democratic Party. This co-ordinated action helped setting the issue of violence against women and domestic violence on the political agenda of cantons where this was not as yet a topic.

The following examples further illustrate the agenda-setting function of the uses of treaties by cantonal MPs. In Zurich (1,537,408 inhabitants in 2021), a series of parliamentary interventions[16] related to the Istanbul Convention was submitted by a group of cantonal MPs from the Social Democratic Party. The first one on 'Violence against women' was partly inspired by the intervention template from the national Social Democratic Party. The goal of these interventions was 'to put the topic on the political agenda, to bring it to the public'.[17] The interventions received media coverage. According to people from the Zurich Intervention Centre against Domestic Violence, the parliamentary interventions put pressure on the government.[18] It is perhaps not a coincidence that shortly after these interventions, on 27 February 2019, the cantonal government decided to include a focus on violence against women in its law enforcement strategy 2019–2022. During our interview, two of these

[13] Interview with a member of the cantonal parliament (Social Democratic Party), Neuchâtel, 5 June 2020.

[14] Interpellation (18.216) 'Istanbul Convention: What about its implementation?' filed by Martine Docourt Ducommun (SP), Cantonal Parliament, Neuchâtel, 11 November 2018. To provide the reader with a sense of the content of each parliamentary intervention, we quote them mentioning their translated title (from French or German).

[15] Interpellation (34/18) 'Violence against women – what does Canton Schwyz?' filed by Carmen Muffler and Jonathan Prelicz (SP), Cantonal Parliament, Schwyz, 5 December 2018.

[16] Question (262/2018) 'Violence against women', filed by Michèle Dünki, Pia Ackermann and Rafael Steiner (SP) 3 September 2018, Statement of the Social Democratic Party on the implementation of the Istanbul Convention filed on 3 December 2018, Question (372/2018) 'Violence against women 2' filed by Pia Ackermann, Sylvie Matter and Michèle Dünki (SP) on 3 December 2018, and Question (374/2019) 'Victim protection for all' filed by Sybille Marti, Michèle Dünki-Bättig and Pia Ackermann (SP) on 25 November 2019. All these parliamentary interventions were filed in Zurich Cantonal Parliament.

[17] Interview with two members of the cantonal parliament (Social Democratic Party), Zurich, 20 January 2021.

[18] Interview with two members of the Zurich Intervention Centre against Domestic Violence, Zurich, 23 April 2021.

cantonal MPs explained that their goal was to put the issue on the political agenda and to press the cantonal government to act but not to specify the concrete measures:

> So, I think it is important to see the following: we are not somehow operationally active in this topic. What we do is try to put the topic on the political agenda, to bring it to the public and thereby also bring about an awareness and visibility for this topic. But quasi operationally or legally [...] that is like not our level, that is done by the administration. And [...] even if we, now for example, demand measures, then we would actually say that. I'll make an example now: we would like an action plan with measures that help to curb violence against women. But we would not somehow already make a legal interpretation or also an operational interpretation, so to speak. We would rather give a general impulse and pressure. And then, so to speak, about the operationalisation of this concern, that would be done by the cantonal administration and the government. I think that there is simply this division of tasks.[19]

The use of the Istanbul Convention in the parliamentary interventions demanding its implementation put political pressure on the cantonal government of Zurich, which subsequently made it a priority theme in its strategy for the 2019–2022 legislative period, and decided to adopt an action plan.[20]

In the case of the CRPD as well, cantonal MPs filed interventions to request information on the implementation of the treaty. In Zurich, three parliamentarians from different political parties filed the question: 'Implementation of the UN Convention on the Rights of Persons with Disabilities by the Canton of Zurich'.[21] In Schwyz, the postulate filed by a cantonal MP of the Social Democratic Party argues that the federal Disability Equality Act and the CRPD require periodic reporting to 'call on the government to provide information on the current disability policy of the Canton of Schwyz in an impact report'.[22]

Besides cantonal MPs, civil society organisations also use parliamentary interventions to put the implementation of the treaties or related issues on the political agenda. Members of civil society organisations can sometimes use parliamentary interventions themselves through a popular motion[23] in the cantons where this instrument is available, or indirectly by asking cantonal MPs to relay a parliamentary intervention, or by helping them write one. This was the case in Neuchâtel, where a CSO—Forum Handicap Neuchâtel—filed

---

[19] Interview with two members of the cantonal parliament from the Social Democratic Party, Zurich, 20 January 2021.

[20] We will detail this type of engagement in Chapter 5.

[21] Translated from German.

[22] Postulate (P 2/20) filed by Leo Camenzind and four co-signatories: 'Is the cantonal disability policy a 'black box' for the cantonal parliament?', Cantonal Parliament, Schwyz, 10 March 2020.

[23] A popular motion is a mandatory order to the cantonal government to send an information report or a report accompanied by a draft law in case of acceptance by the cantonal parliament.

a motion 'For a real cantonal policy on equality for people with disabilities and reduced mobility',[24] which argued that the federal law on the equality for people with disabilities celebrated its tenth year in 2014, and that the CRPD was ratified the same year by Switzerland. In doing so, Forum Handicap Neuchâtel put the issues of the equality for people with disabilities and of the implementation of the CRPD on the cantonal political agenda. The motion was adopted in 2015 and led the cantonal government to prepare a law project with the goal of complying with the CRPD. This led to the adoption of a cantonal law on the inclusion and support of people living with a disability (in French: *Loi sur l'inclusion et l'accompagnement des personnes vivant avec un handicap*) entered into force on 1 January 2022.

Besides agenda-setting, subnational actors use human rights treaties to support claims—sometimes to implement a treaty and sometimes rather as an 'add-on' to support a claim from below.

4.3 USING INTERNATIONAL TREATIES TO SUPPORT CLAIMS

While subnational actors use international treaties to place an issue on the agenda, they often also use treaties to make specific claims, according to their own interests, agendas and strategies. In this section, we will show that cantonal MPs often use treaties, including specific obligations, to support some of their claims in relation to treaty implementation (Sect. 4.3.1). We will show that some of these claims originate from civil society 'on the ground', and that the treaty is used afterwards as an argument or a contextual reference to provide additional weight to a claim (Sect. 4.3.2). Finally, another type of use we observed concerns scenarios in which actors do not make claims for new measures but rather use treaties to legitimise, maintain or strengthen existing ones (Sect. 4.3.3).

4.3.1 Using International Treaties to Support Claims on Specific Treaty Obligations

We observe that cantonal MPs often base their claim on specific obligations of a treaty or ask for the implementation of a specific article. In the case of the Istanbul Convention, in Neuchâtel, cantonal MPs of the Social Democratic Party filed a recommendation[25] which aimed at the provision of a 24-hour hotline for victims of domestic violence based on an obligation related to

---

[24] Popular motion (14.174) filed by Forum Handicap Neuchâtel, 'For a real cantonal policy on equality for people with disabilities and reduced mobility', Cantonal Parliament, Neuchâtel, 3 December 2014.

[25] A recommendation is an invitation to the cantonal government to take action in an area within its regulatory authority.

article 24 of the Istanbul Convention.²⁶ While this demand concerns the implementation of a specific obligation of the IC, subnational actors also use the CRPD to support specific claims or issues that are based on specific treaty provisions. For instance, in a motion filed by Mohamed Hamdaoui (Alliance of the Centre) in the canton of Berne ('For an official recognition of the sign language'), specific articles of the CRPD are quoted to underline a claim about the lack of implementation of the CRPD in the canton:

> Switzerland is one of the last countries in Europe not to have recognised sign language at the national level. At the cantonal level, sign language is mentioned in the constitutions of Geneva and Zurich. This lack of recognition is in contradiction with the UN Convention on the Rights of Persons with Disabilities. In article 2, it defines sign language as a language in its own right. Article 30 (para. 4) of the Convention on the Rights of Persons with Disabilities is even more explicit about deaf language and culture: 'Persons with disabilities have the right, on an equal basis with others, to recognition and support of their specific cultural and linguistic identity, including sign languages and deaf culture.'²⁷

This example shows how a cantonal MP uses the treaty to support a claim and the treaty is the key argument supporting that claim. Similarly, in Zurich, on 12 December 2018, three parliamentarians of the Evangelical People's Party relayed, in a parliamentary question, demands for the implementation of the CRPD made by the Zurich and Schaffhausen sections of the Swiss Association for the Blind and Visually Impaired. The authors of the question used the CRPD (as well as a federal law, the Disability Equality Act of 2004) to ask whether or to what extent the cantonal government was prepared to implement these demands, and if not, to provide a justification.²⁸

Another example of a use of a treaty to support a claim revolving around one of the human rights treaties is an 'urgent written question' filed by a cantonal MP in Geneva. A member of the Social Democratic Party asked the cantonal government about the measures it plans to take concerning treatment plans in psychiatric hospitals and the oversight of the latter to comply with the CRPD (the text quotes art. 16 para. 3 CRPD).²⁹ The cantonal MP uses the treaty to address a very specific and concrete issue. He relied on help from a lawyer working in a CSO with whom the MP was in contact. Thus,

---

[26] Recommendation (21.151), 'Provide a 24-hour hotline for victims of domestic violence', filed by Romain Dubois et al. (SP), Cantonal Parliament, Neuchâtel, 24 March 2021.

[27] Motion (161-2019), 'For an official recognition of the sign language', filed by Mohamed Hamdaoui, Cantonal Parliament, Berne, 11 June 2019.

[28] Question (313/2018) 'Need for action due to the CRPD for visually impaired and blind people', filed by Walter Meier, Tobias Mani and Mark Anthony Wisskirchen (Evangelical People's Party), Cantonal Parliament, Zurich, 12 December 2018.

[29] Question (QUE 772) 'Meeting the requirements of the UN Convention on the Rights of Persons with Disabilities in psychiatric hospitals' filed by Alberto Velasco, Cantonal Parliament, Geneva, 21 February 2018.

the cantonal MP relayed this question to support a claim around the treaty itself and to require specific information from the cantonal government.[30] The cantonal MPs can thus relay claims, questions and demands on concrete issues, sometimes formulated by CSO, and use the treaties as arguments or highlighting obligations within.

These examples show how a treaty can be used by parliamentarians, as well as by civil society organisations (relayed here by cantonal MPs) as a reference to formulate and argue their claims and demands *according to* the treaty. These claims sometimes request the implementation of specific measures and obligations contained in a human rights treaty. In such cases, it is not the implementation of the treaty as a whole that is requested, but specific measures based on (or referring to) the treaty. Thus, specific groups (CSO and their allies in the parliament) use the treaty as a basis for formulating claims (cognitive resource), as a legal reference (sometimes highlighting problems of implementation) to support specific demands (legal resource), and as an argument of authority to place an issue on the political agenda and to urge the cantonal government to act (political resource). Thus, treaties provide important resources to subnational actors committed to a specific cause (gender equality, women's rights, disability rights, human rights) to set the cantonal political agenda and push political authorities to take policy measures or make reforms.

4.3.2 Using International Treaties as an 'Add-on' to Support Claims from Below

Several uses of international treaties by cantonal MPs originate not in the treaties themselves, but from below. Contrary to the uses in the previous section, subnational actors sometimes do not take the treaty as the starting point, but rather as an 'add-on'. In these cases, an issue, a problem or a claim is identified by civil society, or simply observed 'on the ground', and the treaty is used afterwards, i.e. as a later added argument or a contextual reference supporting the construction of the problem and the related claims.

In Geneva, for example, a motion filed by Léna Strasser (Social Democratic Party)—'What if the administration made itself understood by using language that was easy to read and understand?'[31]—referred to the CRPD in the legal background and in the explanatory statement, explaining that:

> Specifically for people with disabilities, it should be noted that the simplified language complies with the UN Convention on the Rights of Persons with Disabilities, which Switzerland ratified in 2014. The treaty requires accessibility

---

[30] Interview with a cantonal MP of the Social Democratic Party, Geneva, 22 March 2022.

[31] Motion (M 2742) 'What if the administration made itself understood by using language that was easy to read and understand?' filed by Léna Strasser et al., Cantonal Parliament Geneva, 5 March 2021.

in all areas of life and therefore accessibility to written information concerning for example health, work, education, practical life, culture, elections, etc.[32]

During the hearing organised by the legislative commission of the cantonal parliament in charge of studying her motion, this cantonal MP explained that the idea of this motion arose during a discussion with associations at the beginning of the school year. The administrative texts concerning the start of the school year were not understandable for the various groups concerned, which led her to look at methods of simplifying the language.[33] In the report of the parliamentary commission, the commission does not mention the CRPD (although a reference figured in the text of her motion). It was only during the hearing of a Head of association by the parliamentary commission that this civil society organisation representative mentioned the CRPD by saying that simplifying language would also make it possible to respect international treaties on persons with disabilities.[34] Thus, in this case, the reference to the CRPD was used as an additional legal argument and a legal background, that supports claims based on statements and needs observed 'on the ground'. The main purpose of this motion was not to implement the treaty but to bring solutions to a problem identified 'on the ground', with the side argument that it would also contribute to strengthening the implementation of the treaty.

Another example of a use of the treaty as an 'add-on' concerns shelters for victims of domestic violence in the canton of Geneva. Two cantonal MPs from the Social Democratic Party requested more shelters for victims of domestic violence. The motion is mainly based on statistics related to domestic violence and on the 'current overcrowding of shelters for victims of domestic violence and their children [which] led to the refusal of 487 applications for protection in 2018, out of a total of 1771 in Switzerland'.[35] The accompanying statement mentions the Istanbul Convention to highlight a 'duty to provide sufficient and dignified shelters for every victim'.[36] During their hearing by the parliamentary commission in charge of studying their motion, the two cantonal MPs quote Article 23 of the Istanbul Convention, which formulates an obligation to provide for the setting-up of shelters in sufficient numbers. The report of the parliamentary commission summarises the stakes as follows:

---

[32] Ibid.

[33] Report (M 2742-A) of the legislative commission in charge of studying the motion of Léna Strasser and others: 'What if the administration made itself understood by using language that was easy to read and understand?', Cantonal Parliament, Geneva, 3 May 2022.

[34] Ibid.

[35] Motion proposal (M 2565) 'For an increase in shelter places for victims of domestic violence', filed by Youniss Mussa, Caroline Marti et al., Cantonal Parliament, Geneva, 20 May 2019.

[36] Ibid.

Ms. Marti recalls that Switzerland has made a number of commitments concerning the fight against domestic violence and this at the level of the Council of Europe Convention on preventing and combating violence against women and domestic violence. Article 23 stipulates that its signatory members must take measures to ensure appropriate and sufficient accommodation that guarantees the safety of victims. Article 26 states that the rights and needs of children who are affected by such violence if they are with a parent must be taken into account.[37]

However, as the two parliamentarians who wrote this motion explained to us, 'the primary objective was not to implement the Istanbul Convention'.[38] The writing of this motion took place some weeks before the 2019 Women's Strike in Switzerland (14 June 2019). In this context, these two members of the cantonal parliament aimed at bringing 'part of the claims [of this mobilisation] to the [cantonal parliament]'. The manifesto of the collective of the Women's Strike included claims for gender equality, but also protection of women against violence. So, the two cantonal MPs studied the situation in Geneva and realised 'that there was a very critical situation in this field, with a rather cruel lack of accommodation places and of emergency accommodation'.[39] They worked on the text of their motion with a parliamentary assistant who found the Istanbul Convention:

> [...] we had some elements to show that there were needs, but also in terms of legal and moral obligations on the part of the State and it is there [at this stage], to be completely transparent, it is our parliamentary assistant who found ... well who came across this Istanbul Convention to which Switzerland is bound. And there you have it, it is a rather strong argument to show that there is a need, especially a need for Switzerland and the cantons to act in these areas.[40]

Hence, even if what this motion requests matches with an obligation of the treaty, the use of the treaty occurred a bit haphazardly during an ongoing attempt to formulate a specific claim. The authors did not primarily seek to implement the treaty as one of them explains:

> There is no real in-depth work [from us] in relation to the Istanbul Convention, to be honest. The Istanbul Convention is cited to support the fact that

---

[37] Report (M 2565-A) of the Social Affairs Committee charged with studying the proposed motion by Youniss Mussa, Caroline Marti et al. 'For an increase in shelter places for victims of domestic violence' (*translated from French*), Cantonal Parliament of Geneva, 20 April 2020.

[38] Interview, with a cantonal MP from the Social Democratic Party, Geneva, 6 October 2020.

[39] Ibid.

[40] Ibid.

Switzerland has commitments, particularly with regard to the issue of domestic violence.[41]

Hence, the treaty is used here as a support and an argument for a claim that comes from the field, and which matches an obligation of the treaty. This shows the specific 'force' (Bourdieu, 1987) of a treaty, and of international law, which imbues demands and claims with the legitimacy and incontestability of 'superior law'. Subnational actors use treaties in this way when the obligations are used not just to emphasise a need, but when the actors also want to flag a legal responsibility to take specific actions or measures. In short, this motion was mainly based on the goal to bring claims of the Women's Strike to the parliament and on an observation of concrete problems 'on the ground' (the insufficient places for victims of domestic violence in shelters). The use of the Istanbul Convention, and more specifically its Article 23, was an opportunity—that they came to know of 'on the go', working on the text of their motion—to add an additional argument supporting their claims.

4.3.3 Using Treaties as Legitimation Tools for Existing Claims

Where some implementation has occurred, the implementation of a treaty is never written in stone. When the subnational authorities in cantons in the past took measures, these measures and notably the financial means to sustain them can later continue to be contested. Specialised policy bureaucrats then sometimes use treaties to legitimise existing measures. In other cantons, specialised policy bureaucrats can also use treaties to reinforce or further develop an already-existing policy.

We observe this type of use in French-speaking cantons in regard to the Istanbul Convention. This is so because the services responsible for this domain are 'Gender Equality Offices', while in German-speaking cantons and Ticino (Italian-speaking), these are 'specialised or co-ordination offices against domestic violence' in departments of police, security, interior or social services. In the cantons where the public problem of violence against women and domestic violence was already framed as a problem linked to gender equality as intended by the Istanbul Convention, and where gender equality offices previously promoted public policies in this direction (Delage et al., 2020; Roca i Escoda & Lieber, 2015), the IC came 'to clarify certain points and at the same time to legitimise everything that had been done until then, which seemed right, which seemed to be going in the right direction'.[42] One equality delegate also underlines that the IC not only legitimises the framing of a public problem and a policy approach, but it also provides a status of priority by

---

[41] Interview with a cantonal MP from the Social Democratic Party, Geneva, 1 October 2020.

[42] Interview with the Head of the Cantonal Office for Family Policy and Equality, Neuchâtel, 13 March 2020.

strengthening the argument according to which there is a necessity to take policy measures in this domain. International law has a specific 'force' as an argument of authority.

> And then the Istanbul Convention is a good way to reinforce the message on the need to implement measures that respond to the needs of victims, perpetrators, children concerned and whether it is in terms of promotion of awareness measures and concrete care for different people (...) and the Istanbul Convention gives a stronger foundation, it is not just the will of a cantonal equality office or feminist associations, or this, or that association. It's really society as a whole.[43]

This example shows that in those cantons in which 'Gender Equality Offices' are in charge of the issues around domestic violence and violence against women, the IC gave legitimacy to ideas that already existed, and reinforced the policy path that was already taken. The treaty provided an opportunity to strengthen the message on the need to implement measures in this field in the various directions set by the IC: prevention of all forms of violence, protection of victims from further violence, prosecution of perpetrators, and co-ordinated policies. In cantons in which the subject matter of the Istanbul Convention is perceived as mostly an issue of police and justice, the same type of use of the treaty could not be observed.

Chapter 5 will present the sequel stories to those uses which have led to the engagement of the relevant subnational political authorities with the treaties and we will categorise patterns of this engagement. However, as mentioned in Chapter 1, subnational actors regularly use treaties without the later engagement of the political authorities. At the end of Chapter 5, we will summarise the favouring and limiting factors and the potential that a use of a treaty by a subnational actor succeeds in stimulating the authorities' engagement.

4.4 Discussion and Conclusion

This chapter presented the variety of uses of treaties by actors at the subnational level. The two studied human rights treaties are used (a) to set an issue on the cantonal political agenda and (b) to support new or existing claims. The actors using treaties thereby try to push for the engagement of the subnational political authorities with the treaty and ultimately the adoption of policy measures. Treaties like the IC and the CRPD can be used as a tool in political struggles to contest, reform or improve local norms regarding disability, gender equality or violence against women and domestic violence. As Heyer shows about the CRPD in Germany and Japan, the adoption of the CRPD 'offered a new arena for activists to draw attention to those rights and to put pressure on their governments to enact reforms' (Heyer, 2015, p. 204),

---

[43] Interview with the Head of the Cantonal Office for the Promotion of Equality and Prevention of Violence, Geneva, 1 July 2020.

and provided 'a powerful awareness-raising tool for activists' (Heyer, 2015, p. 209). We confirm these observations in our two case studies, extending the analysis made for activists to specialised policy bureaucrats and parliamentarians who are committed to a cause (gender equality, women's rights, disability rights) (Bereni, 2021; Bereni & Revillard, 2018; Childs & Krook, 2009; Revillard, 2019; Vanhala, 2011). Thus, while human rights treaties could a priori be conceived as constraints to subnational authorities, they also open a 'window of opportunity' (Kingdon, 2014) to actors for whom using a treaty—as a whole, or with specific obligations—matches with their own interests. Certain specialised bureaucrats use treaties to legitimise existing policies and the approach that they promoted so far, i.e. their framing of the public problem (Brown, 2018; Delage et al., 2020). This legitimation enables them to further develop the existing policies in the path already taken—placing reforms and new measures on the political agenda, and requesting additional resources –, and to strengthen their leading and co-ordinating position as well as their legitimacy as a policy focal point in the field of public policy (Bourdieu, 1994; Dubois, 2012), i.e. in their relations with the other actors involved in a policy process.[44]

Subnational parliamentarians also make a variety of uses of treaties: requesting their implementation or measures to comply with specific obligations, mobilising them as legal and political arguments to support their claims, building them on the basis of the treaty (cognitive resource). The members of cantonal parliaments who use treaties are the most often committed to a cause (equality's and women's cause, disability rights' cause, human rights). In this sense, they use the treaty to advance their cause's interests, also because the treaty matches with these interests. In doing so, they can be analysed as international law intermediaries (more specifically agenda-setting intermediaries), performing an intermediary function (Pélisse, 2019; Talesh & Pélisse, 2019) between the global and local levels by translating and using international treaties in subnational policymaking processes, as we demonstrated elsewhere (Miaz et al., 2024).

The two studied human rights treaties provide important legal, political and cognitive resources to subnational actors to set an issue on the agenda, to frame a public problem, to argue their claims and to impulse policy processes (for a summary, see Table 4.1). Studying how actors refer to treaties, we also observe that their uses are not predetermined by some systematic legal analysis, but rather are pragmatic and crafty.

Human rights treaties can support subnational actors to make the most of their agency. Despite the usually very significant distance between subnational actors and those who made the international treaties, subnational actors can

---

[44] In the case of the Istanbul Convention and the policy preventing and combating violence against women and domestic violence, these other actors can be the police, judges, health professionals, social workers, associations, CSOs and other frontline workers in this domain (in shelters, in centres or programmes for perpetrators of domestic violence), etc.

Table 4.1 Variety of uses of human rights treaties (summary)

Types of uses	Description/Actions	Actors	Venues/Arenas
Using treaties for agenda-setting			
Institutional agenda-setting	Specialised policy bureaucrats self-process and place the implementation of a treaty (or specific issues and obligations within) on their institutional agenda They prepare proposals (legislative reform, action plan, specific measures, budgets)	Specialised policy bureaucrats	Bureaucracy
Placing the implementation of the treaty on the political agenda	By requesting information on, or claiming for the implementation of a treaty, actors place this issue on the cantonal political agenda	Cantonal MPs CSOs Specialised policy bureaucrats	Parliament; Government
Placing a specific issue or obligation on the political agenda	Actors use the reference to a treaty to place a specific issue or an obligation of the treaty on the political agenda. This can be achieved by: Requesting information Claiming for specific measures Highlighting a specific obligation	Cantonal MPs CSOs Specialised policy bureaucrats Academic experts	Parliament; Government
Using the reference to the treaty to support claims or proposals	Reference to the treaty or to an obligation (a specific one, or the duty to comply with the treaty) to support and argue claims or proposals	Cantonal MPs CSOs	Parliament; Government

(continued)

Table 4.1 (continued)

Types of uses	Description/Actions	Actors	Venues/Arenas
Using treaties to support (new or existing) claims			
Legitimising the existing policy/path	Symbolic uses and symbolic impact on policy and on the position of specialised bureaucracies in the field concerned by the treaty	Specialised policy bureaucrats	Bureaucracy; Government
Cognitive resource	The treaty provides a cognitive resource to frame and approach certain issues (construction of public problems)	Specialised policy bureaucrats Cantonal government Academic experts Cantonal MPs CSOs People	Bureaucracy; Government; 'on the ground' (street-level)
Street-level resource	Symbolic, legal and cognitive resource of bureaucrats, civil society and street-level organisations in street-level work	Specialised policy bureaucrats Street-level organisations CSOs	Bureaucracy; 'on the ground' (street-level)

make active use of these obligations, by adapting them to the local context in accordance with their goals and interests.

However, not all actors are equal. The role of legislators in taking the first steps leading up to an engagement is relatively marginal, as they are rarely proactive or directly in charge in that regard (Niederhauser & Maggetti, 2023). Instead, specialised policy bureaucrats are particularly prominent at different stages observed in Swiss cantonal policy processes. A small number of them, sometimes single individuals,—those with competencies, expertise, information, motivation and some resources—stand out as key players, who are able to use human rights treaties in accordance with their strategy. At the same time, the ultimate impact of these strategies is highly dependent on the political context of the subnational unit at stake, and in particular on the degree of favourableness of the political majority within cantonal political institutions. In this chapter, we have focused the analysis on subnational *uses* of international treaties. In the next chapter, we show through which patterns uses of the treaty often result in engagement, i.e. political authorities taking policy and law measures as a result of the treaty.

References

Bereni, L. (2021). The Women's Cause in a Field: Rethinking the Architecture of Collective Protest in the Era of Movement Institutionalization. *Social Movement Studies, 20*(2), 208–223. https://doi.org/10.1080/14742837.2019.1679107

Bereni, L., & Revillard, A. (2018). Movement Institutions: The Bureaucratic Sources of Feminist Protest. *Politics & Gender, 14*(3), 407–432. https://doi.org/10.1017/S1743923X18000399

Bourdieu, P. (1987). The Force of Law: Toward a Sociology of the Juridical Field (Translated by Richard Terdiman). *The Hastings Law Journal, 38*(5), 805–853.

Bourdieu, P. (1994). Rethinking the State: Genesis and Structure of the Bureaucratic Field. *Sociological Theory, 12*(1), 1. https://doi.org/10.2307/202032

Brown, G. (2018). De la « violence masculine » à la « gestion des menaces ». Judiciarisation des violences et euphémisation des rapports sociaux de sexe. *Droit et société, 99*(2), 357–371.

Childs, S., & Krook, M. L. (2009). Analysing Women's Substantive Representation: From Critical Mass to Critical Actors. *Government and Opposition, 44*(2), 125–145. https://doi.org/10.1111/j.1477-7053.2009.01279.x

Delage, P., Lieber, M., & Roca i Escoda, M. (2020). *Contrer les violences dans le couple: émergence et reconfigurations d'un problème public*. Antipodes.

Dubois, V. (2012). The Fields of Public Policy. In M. Hilgers & E. Mangez (Eds.), *Social Field Theory: Concept and Applications* (pp. 199–220). Routledge.

Guaschino, E. (2023). *Regulators as Agenda-Setters. How National Agencies Shape Public Issues*. Routledge.

Heyer, K. (2015). *Rights Enabled: The Disability Revolutionl, from the US, to Germany and Japan, to the United Nations*. University of Michigan Press.

Kaempfer, C. (2023). *Les mécanismes de mise en oeuvre du droit international par les cantons suisses: études de cas dans les domaines des droits humains et des accords bilatéraux Suisse-UE*. Sui generis.

Kingdon, J. W. (2014). *Agendas, Alternatives, and Public Policies* (2nd ed., Pearson New International Edition ed.). Pearson.

Merry, S. E. (2006). *Human Rights and Gender Violence: Translating International Law into Local Justice*. University of Chicago Press.

Miaz, J., Niederhauser, M., & Maggetti, M. (2024). From International Law to Subnational Practices: The Roles of Intermediaries in Translating the Istanbul Convention in Swiss Cantons. *Regulation & Governance, 18*(1), 121–128. https://doi.org/10.1111/rego.12523

Niederhauser, M., & Maggetti, M. (2023). Multi-level Implementation of International Law: The Role of Vertical Epistemic Communities. *Swiss Political Science Review, 29*(4), 299–321.

Page, E. C. (2012). *Policy Without Politicians: Bureaucratic Influence in Comparative Perspective*. Oxford University Press.

Page, E. C., & Jenkins, B. (2005). *Policy Bureaucracy*. Oxford University Press.

Pélisse, J. (2019). Varieties of Legal Intermediaries: When Non-Legal Professionals Act as Legal Intermediaries. *Studies in Law, Politics and Society, 81*, 101–128.

Revillard, A. (2019). Realizing the Right to Access in France: Between Implementation and Activation. *Law & Society Review, 53*(4), 950–982.

Roca i Escoda, M., & Lieber, M. (2015). La mise en oeuvre et les mutations d'un problème public: Les violences faites aux femmes dans le Canton de Genève. *Oñati Socio-legal Series, 5*(2), 766–784.

Talesh, S., & Pélisse, J. (2019). How Legal Intermediaries Facilitate or Inhibit Social Change. *Studies in Law, Politics, and Society, 79*, 111–145.

Vanhala, L. (2011). *Making Rights a Reality?* Cambridge University Press.

Open Access This chapter is licensed under the terms of the Creative Commons Attribution 4.0 International License (http://creativecommons.org/licenses/by/4.0/), which permits use, sharing, adaptation, distribution and reproduction in any medium or format, as long as you give appropriate credit to the original author(s) and the source, provide a link to the Creative Commons license and indicate if changes were made.

The images or other third party material in this chapter are included in the chapter's Creative Commons license, unless indicated otherwise in a credit line to the material. If material is not included in the chapter's Creative Commons license and your intended use is not permitted by statutory regulation or exceeds the permitted use, you will need to obtain permission directly from the copyright holder.

CHAPTER 5

The Different Ways in Which Subnational Political Authorities Engage with International Human Rights Treaties

Abstract Engagement with human rights treaties occurs when the political authorities of a subnational unit try to understand an international treaty and intend to take policy measures to deal with it with a view to its (further) implementation. Our results indicate that there are three different ways in which political authorities engage with treaties: implementation-centred engagement, initiating engagement and embedded engagement. We base this typology on examples from our two case studies on the Istanbul Convention (IC) and the Convention on the Rights of Persons with Disabilities (CRPD), providing a granular understanding of what happens when subnational authorities commit to deal with a human rights treaty. At the end of this chapter, we discuss the conditions favouring and limiting the chances that the uses of treaties succeed in stimulating the engagement of political authorities and we offer a comparative outlook to distil similarities and differences in the patterns of engagement of subnational political authorities with the Istanbul Convention and the CRPD.

Keywords Engagement of subnational political authorities with treaties · Human rights treaties · Implementation · Specialised Policy Bureaucrats · Subnational Parliaments

5.1 Introduction

We saw in Chapter 4 how subnational actors use international human rights treaties in several ways in subnational policy processes. This chapter now looks at how subnational political authorities engage with them. As explained in Chapter 1, engagement occurs when the political authorities (i.e. parliament and government) of a given subnational jurisdiction intend to take policy and legislative measures to deal with an international treaty with a view of (further) implementing it. When subnational actors use human rights treaties, these uses can stimulate further uses by other actors and sometimes the engagement of the political authorities. Understanding and systematising the patterns of such engagement is the objective of this chapter. Exploring these patterns of engagement shows how international human rights treaties stimulate dynamic policy processes, involving various uses of the treaties that interact with each other, leading subnational political authorities to take measures that ultimately result in often self-reinforcing policy changes. Consistent with previous research on human rights implementation and internalisation (Donald & Speck, 2020; Haglund & Stryker, 2015; Risse et al., 1999), we show that engaging with international human rights treaties is an iterative, non-linear process, which does not stop when measures are taken. Our results also indicate that an evolution or a change of policy approach may occur when subnational authorities commit to engage substantively and treaties can become a cognitive framework of reference in a given public policy field (Dubois, 2012), i.e. actors of this policy field (specialised policy bureaucrats, frontline workers, CSOs, social movements and activists, people concerned) increasingly refer to the treaty not only as a legal reference, but also as a cognitive one to (re)frame their work, the public policy, but also their needs, claims and expectations.

Engaging with a treaty does not guarantee its ultimate implementation but denotes a key shift when political authorities take a step towards a treaty's implementation. We invite readers to refer to Chapter 1 where we elaborate on the relationship between engagement, implementation and compliance. Studying the variety of uses of a treaty offered us important clues to understand how the engagement of political authorities with a treaty comes about. The next step is now to analyse the different patterns (or types) of engagement as a better understanding of such engagement will provide valuable information on the subsequent implementation processes.

We will proceed as follows. We will identify three different patterns of engagement—according to the weight given to the human rights treaty in the process, the goals of the policy process, the types of measures taken, and the types of cantonal trajectories (existing measures and policymaking process).

5.2 PATTERNS OF ENGAGEMENT

Based on our two case studies on the Istanbul Convention and the CRPD in Swiss cantonal jurisdictions, the first pattern we observed is an engagement of the political authorities that aims at implementing the treaty either 'as a whole' or by focusing on at least one specific issue (Sect. 5.2.1). Second, we introduce the concept of initiating engagement, which we observed in cantons that lack existing measures in the policy domain and have generalist administrations (typically the Social Affairs Office). In such cases, these administrations require additional resources to actively initiate engagement with the treaty (Sect. 5.2.2). Third, embedded engagement occurs when the treaty is used as a cognitive, legal, or political resource alongside other resources. In this case, engagement with the treaty or parts thereof occurs as part of a broader project that extends beyond or alongside the specific issue covered by the treaty and whose main goals are not directly related to implement the treaty or specific obligations (Sect. 5.2.4). These patterns of engagement can sometimes overlap.

5.2.1 Implementation-Centred Engagement

The first, main and most frequent pattern of engagement is an implementation-centred engagement, i.e. an engagement that aims at implementing the treaty. In this pattern, subnational political authorities (i.e. parliament and government) take legislative (new law, legislative reform) and/or other policy measures (action plans) with a view to (further) implementing the treaty. This pattern of engagement is often a progressive, 'step-by-step', process opening a policy path. Implementation-centred engagement involves taking stock of the existing measures and often begins with an identification of the needs on the ground. Implementation-centred engagement revolves around the idea that a treaty or a specific aspect or obligation contained therein must be implemented, in other words, the treaty is the starting point.

How does implementation-centred engagement come about? The process leading to an implementation-centred engagement can involve multiple steps and often passes through one or the other mechanisms described in Chapter 3, and the combination of uses of the treaty by other actors tends to result in a stronger level of engagement. Through this process, a new policy orientation may emerge, with the treaty gradually becoming integrated into the common cognitive framework of policymakers and gaining prominence. Implementation-centred engagement involves political authorities adopting a policy path that takes the treaty as a starting point. This path may either reinforce an existing approach or give rise to a new paradigm or direction inspired by the treaty.

We distinguish two sub-types of implementation-centred engagement: law reform and action plans. The first approach involves enacting new legislation or revising existing laws to align with the treaty's obligations (Sect. 5.2.1.1). The second approach is bureaucratic in nature, where the authorities develop an action plan to co-ordinate and organise public policy efforts and new measures in the relevant field (Sect. 5.2.1.3). Both approaches can be accompanied by the allocation of additional financial resources and the creation of new positions or institutions to oversee and co-ordinate the implementation of the new law or action plan.

First, we will now turn to implementation-centred engagement in the form of legislative measures, either to implement a treaty as a whole or a specific issue.

5.2.1.1 The Legislative Way: A New Law or a Law Reform to Implement the Treaty as a Whole

Implementation-centred engagement with a treaty can be achieved through the adoption of new legislation or adapting existing ones. In these processes, law is an instrument of the implementation of a treaty. In these cases, the need for implementing the treaty is the main argument supporting the legal changes. The following legislative reform in the canton of Neuchâtel illustrates this type of implementation-centred engagement.

The political authorities in Neuchâtel engaged with the Istanbul Convention when they started the process of what became a new law on domestic violence adopted in November 2019.[1] The authorities initiated the law reform to align the existing legislation with the requirements of the Istanbul Convention. As mentioned in Chapter 4, the cantonal Equality Delegate played a decisive role by using the Istanbul Convention to support her draft legislation. She convinced the Cantonal Minister responsible for her office to present draft legislation to the cantonal parliament and the report that she prepared mentioned that the Istanbul Convention 'opens a new era in the fight against [violence against women and domestic violence]', and that the canton 'will be able to honour its obligations coming from the signature of the Istanbul Convention'.[2] To the Equality Delegate, 'the Istanbul Convention is actually more adapted to today's times'[3] and brings new definitions and new measures in this policy domain. Furthermore, 'the Istanbul Convention makes a very clear link between domestic violence and inequality'.[4] As we explained in Chapter 4, the Equality Delegate was able to use the Istanbul Convention to support her draft legislation, strengthening the framing of the issues of domestic violence and violence against women that was already present in the

---

[1] Canton of Neuchâtel, *Loi sur la lutte contre la violence domestique* of 5 November 2019, 322.05, https://rsn.ne.ch/DATA/program/books/RSN2021/20211/htm/32205.htm.

[2] Cantonal government of Neuchâtel, «*Rapport du Conseil d'État au Grand Conseil à l'appui d'un projet de loi sur la lutte contre la violence domestique*», Neuchâtel, 2019, p. 1 and 24.

[3] Interview with the Head of the Office for Family Policy and Gender Equality, Neuchâtel, 13 March 2020.

[4] Ibid.

cantonal policy. This use developed into an implementation-centred engagement by the political authorities. A lawyer involved in the preparation of the law recounts how the specialised bureaucrats considered the treaty against the background of existing legislation and their options to present a draft law to the cantonal legislator:

> Are we complying with the [Istanbul] Convention or not? What could we implement? And then there was already the law on the fight against violence in couples and this Istanbul Convention was the opportunity to extend the field of application of this law on violence.[5]

Thanks to the subnational political authorities' commitment to engage with the Istanbul Convention, the administration started the process by comparing the existing cantonal law on violence in couple relationships[6] with the IC. As the existing policy already related to several aspects of the IC, the main adaptations concerned the definitions of the types of violence to be addressed and the scope of law (the scope of the former law on 'violence in couple relationships' had to be changed to the notion of 'domestic violence' used in the IC, which is a more global concept, including persons who are no longer in a relationship, and children). Also, by linking domestic violence to gender inequalities, the Istanbul Convention 'gave legitimacy to ideas that already existed'.[7] Thus, the IC played a crucial role in how the issue of domestic violence was framed in this law-making process.

The cantonal administration drafted a report presenting the draft law to the cantonal parliament and explaining that the aim of the new law was to align with the Istanbul Convention. The relevant parliamentary commission relied on this report. During parliamentary debates, cantonal MPs widely supported the draft law. The cantonal parliament of Neuchâtel unanimously adopted the draft law with only minor changes.

This example shows how an international treaty can prompt subnational political authorities to change, support, or reinforce a particular framing and approach to a public issue, leading them to adopt instruments and legal definitions that align with this approach. In doing so, the subnational political authorities engage with the treaty with a view to its (enhanced) implementation.[8]

---

[5] Interview with a former lawyer of the Office for Family Policy and Gender Equality, Neuchâtel, 25 June 2020.

[6] Canton of Neuchâtel, *Loi sur la lutte contre la violence dans les relations de couple (LVCouple)* 30 March 2004 (no longer in force), https://rsn.ne.ch/DATA/program/books/RSN2017/20171/htm/32205.htm.

[7] Interview with the Head of the Office for Family Policy and Gender Equality, Neuchâtel, 13 March 2020.

[8] We should speak, at this stage, about a *partial* implementation, because this legislative reform only concerns domestic violence and not, more generally, violence against women.

Similar implementation-centred engagement was seen with the CRPD. However, unlike the IC example, the CRPD's aims and approach differ from existing cantonal policies as the treaty calls for a revision of the understanding of disability. The CRPD advances the social model of disability (Heyer, 2015; Oliver, 2009), i.e. the treaty understands disability as a condition resulting from a structural problem preventing people with disabilities from carrying out their usual activities in the environment around them (Hess-Klein, 2017). Disability is thus defined as a relative and evolving reality that arises or disappears depending on the environment's ability to adapt to the needs of the person affected (Barnes, 2019). Given that Switzerland still has a predominantly medical conception of disability, the cantons must undertake significant legislative reforms to move towards a social and human rights-based understanding of disability.[9]

Recently, four cantons (Basel-Stadt, Basel-Landschaft, Neuchâtel, Valais) adopted new laws on the rights and inclusion of persons with disabilities aiming at implementing the CRPD, while at least two other cantons (Geneva, Vaud) started a similar law-making process, and two other ones (Berne, Zurich) adopted laws on services for people with disabilities that aimed to change the support system according to the CRPD. The political authorities in the canton of Basel-Stadt were the first to engage with the CRPD in an implementation-centred way. As we will see, their engagement played a role in the subsequent engagement of political authorities in other cantons. In this canton (191,395 inhabitants in 2021), cantonal MPs filed a motion asking the government to draft a law ensuring equality for persons with disabilities, mentioning the CRPD in the very first sentence.[10] In 2017, citizens asked for a new constitutional provision on equality for people with disabilities. They could do so with the tool of a popular initiative (that is, an instrument of direct democracy allowing citizens to propose constitutional changes).[11] The popular initiative explicitly called for the implementation of the CRPD. The cantonal parliament adopted the new law on the rights of persons with disabilities on 18 September 2019.[12] Academic experts and members of the umbrella association of Swiss organisations for people with disabilities were invited to comment on the draft legislation. Other cantons subsequently mandated the same experts to support them in drafting a law reform or a new law. The implementation-centred engagement of the political

---

Nevertheless, this first step was later followed by the adoption of an action plan, which pursued the canton's implementation-centred engagement with the IC (see hereafter).

[9] UN Committee on the Rights of Persons with Disabilities, Concluding Observations on Switzerland, CRPD/C/CHE/CO/1, 13 April 2022, para. 7.

[10] Motion (15.5282.01) 'Cantonal disability equality law', filed by Georg Mattmüller (Social Democratic Party) et al., Cantonal Parliament, Basel-Stadt, 16 September 2015.

[11] Popular Initiative in the Canton of Basel-Stadt, 'For a cantonal disability equality', http://behindertengleichstellung.ch/.

[12] Canton of Basel-Stadt, *Gesetz über die Rechte von Menschen mit Behinderungen*, 18 September 2019.

authorities and the adopted law in Basel-Stadt thus served as a successful example of good practice to engage with the CRPD and this facilitated further uses of the treaty by other actors as well as further engagement by the political authorities in other cantons. We qualify this example as implementation-centred engagement as the treaty serves as the main starting point and argument for legislative reform. As we observed for uses of treaties by subnational actors, engagement by political authorities of one canton can lead to uses and engagement elsewhere as well, which is well-illustrated by this example.

In two other cantons where new laws on the rights and inclusion of persons with disabilities were adopted and in two others where a legislative process is still ongoing,[13] the same group of experts analysed the existing legislation, and proposed not only a framework law, but also legal changes in other cantonal existing laws. The experts proposed a legal analysis of the CRPD and helped parliaments and administrations to understand what their obligations were, and how they can implement the treaty. As one of these experts explained to us:

> It is clear to [most parliaments and also administrations] that something has to be done. But the complexity in this field prevents them from moving forward and they need explanations. And this is something that we often notice when we talk to people from the administration that […] they don't know what their obligations are. They are unsure how to do it. […] So they need help. And so that's what we do. We help them clarify what their obligations are.[14]

When political authorities of a canton are willing to engage with a treaty in an implementation-centred way, academic and civil society experts can play a key role to facilitate the implementation process. The experts proposed to the cantons to adopt a framework law on the rights of persons with disabilities which is very general, but contains the central aspects of the treaty and, importantly, is designed to lead to later uses of the treaty by a range of subnational actors, including the concerned individuals, contributing to a dynamic of further implementation.

> It's all the issues that affect the whole administration, the whole legal system. So, these are the things that we propose to put in a framework law. So [the framework law] is very, very general. And if you look at the framework law that the canton of Basel has made, or also the canton of Valais, the revised law. So, these are general issues, but it is a concretisation of the rights that are in the

---

[13] One of the key experts, Professor Markus Schefer of the University of Basel, has listed the cantons in which he and his team have been involved in 'convincing Cantons to draft such legislation, and (….) intimately involved in writing and – in some Cantons – passing and implementing such legislation': Website of Markus Schefer, 'Advising Cantonal Governments in Switzerland on Implementing the CRPD', https://www.markusschefer.ch/en/work/legislative-activities-54.html.

[14] Interview with an academic scholar and expert, 22 February 2022.

CRPD and this is important. Because it is precisely an experience that people with disabilities make. Without a law, not much happens. And there, especially when there is a subjective right, they have something in hand to make things move and to ask that their rights be implemented effectively. And that is the importance of these framework laws. And so, the framework law is very general, but precisely with very important principles and then, on the other hand, all the sectoral laws, the special laws, as we say, that is another field and normally we should also look at all the laws, to see if they comply with the CRPD.[15]

The experts take the binding legal nature of the treaty obligations as their starting point and identify the international obligations of the cantons to propose new laws and legal modifications aiming at implementing these obligations.

We tell them (the cantons) what the CRPD says and what their obligations are. And these are legal obligations. We explain, we give them explanations. We highlight what other countries are doing, what the committee says on the issue and we try to make them understand that they are obliged to do something.[16]

When a commitment to engage with the treaty exists, such input has proven to be of high practical relevance. Several cantonal parliaments unanimously adopted legislative changes and those changes came with several innovations and new resources for the disability policy of the cantons, all of which allow for further uses of the CRPD by subnational actors.

The canton of Valais offers another example of implementation-centred engagement. In the canton of Valais (346,562 inhabitants), the Head of the Office for the Co-ordination of Social Institutions[17]—started a reform of the 'Law for the *Integration* of Persons with Disabilities'[18] into a 'Law on the Rights and *Inclusion* of Persons with Disabilities'. The legislative reform started from the administration: 'we decided we wanted to do something'. There too, we qualify the engagement with the treaty as implementation-centred, with the treaty at its core. The Head of Office 'saw what [was] happening in other places in Switzerland', like in Basel-Stadt. She explains that the existing law 'was already quite good'.[19] However:

---

[15] Ibid.

[16] Ibid.

[17] Since the law reform, this office is now called 'Office for the Co-ordination of Disability Issues'.

[18] Canton of Valais, *Loi sur l'intégration des personnes handicapées* 31 January 1991 (now entitled *Loi sur les droits et l'inclusion des personnes en situation de handicap*), for the old version, see https://lex.vs.ch/app/fr/texts_of_law/850.6/versions/2176 and for the new one in force since 1 January 2022: https://lex.vs.ch/app/fr/texts_of_law/850.6.

[19] Interview with the Head of the Co-ordinating Office for Disability Issues, Social Action Department, Valais, 23 March 2022.

[…] There was not this part of rights for people with disabilities [that the CRPD requires]. And then, in order to have a law that also corresponds to the demand of the UN, we contacted the University of Basel, Professor Schefer and his team, and we asked them to propose us a partial revision of our law to integrate it in our law.[20]

In comparison with the legislative processes in Basel-Stadt, where the starting point was a motion and a popular initiative, this legislative process thus started in the bureaucracy. The legislative process again involved academic experts as well as a support group composed of representatives of cantonal institutions and civil society. The responsible department of the cantonal administration organised a 'World Café' (an interactive discussion format) with the help of a local association, *Forum Handicap Valais*, to 'include people with disabilities and their relatives in the reflection process related to the modification of the legal bases that concern them.'[21] The event aimed to facilitate discussions on the legislative modifications that concern people with disabilities, and to identify actions and projects that could enhance their quality of life. The president of *Forum Handicap Valais*, who is also a member of the Social Democratic Party in the cantonal parliament, explained how the involvement of those directly concerned was important for the later engagement of the authorities with the treaty:

> because finally, [persons with disabilities] had the impression that it was the first time that we were going to ask them directly what they thought. [Because] when we talk about disability, we tend, at least until now, to go and discuss with the directors of institutions, heads of service, of some services for disability, but finally do they come to ask us? Well, until a few months ago, at least, that was not the case. So, there is this whole notion, they make a law for us, but they don't come to consult us, before this process.[22]

The 'World Café' allowed the identification of the needs and experiences of people most directly concerned and the cantonal political authorities reaffirmed their commitment to implementation-centred engagement with the CRPD. The academic experts then prepared a 'draft law with comments' in July 2020, which served as a basis for the legislative revision. Compared to the existing cantonal law prior to the reform, the legal framework underwent significant changes, which included the addition of a new chapter titled 'Rights

---

[20] Ibid.

[21] Cantonal department of Health, Social Affairs and Culture, Social Action Service, 'Results World Café 'Handicap Valais' 2019. Preparation of the partial Revision of the Valais Law on the Integration of People with Disabilities, in collaboration with the people concerned', Valais, February 2020.

[22] Interview with a cantonal MP from the Social Democratic Party and president of Forum Handicap Valais, 8 April 2022.

of Persons with Disabilities'.[23] Additionally, the office responsible for coordinating disability issues was renamed 'Office of Co-ordination for Disability Issues'. The law's primary objective, which was previously to promote the integration of persons with disabilities, was redefined to emphasise the realisation of the rights of persons with disabilities in all areas of society. The drafters also adjusted the uses of the term 'disability' or 'handicap' to reflect a view that disability is a product of social and societal barriers, rather than merely an impairment. The legal terminology was accordingly adjusted to reflect this change. Finally, the implementation of the legal changes called for the creation of a specialised centre for the rights of persons with disabilities, which required additional means (one full-time employee).

In the cantonal parliament, the parliamentary Commission on Health, Social Affairs and Integration dealt with the draft partial revision of the law. The commission made some modifications and adopted the revision with ten voices for, two against and no abstention. Finally, the cantonal parliament unanimously approved the legislative modifications after the first reading. This example of cantonal engagement with the CRPD thus started from the specialised policy bureaucracy—with the approval of the cantonal government—and involved experts, civil society and people with disabilities. It is an implementation-centred engagement because the CRPD was at the core of the process which finally led to a legislative amendment accepted by the cantonal parliament.

To summarise, introducing legislative reforms with the aim of aligning with a treaty represents an implementation-centred engagement with the treaty. This engagement can be initiated by the uses of the treaties by specialised bureaucrats (Chapter 4) or civil society, and it often benefits from the participation of diverse actors. Regardless of who initiates or participates in the process, the parliament and government—as subnational political authorities—engage with the treaty by adopting the new law or legislative reform.

5.2.1.2 Issue-Specific Engagement: A Sub-Type of Implementation-Centred Engagement

Within the implementation-centred engagement, which we mainly constructed to refer to cases in which the main goal of the law project is to implement a treaty 'as a whole' (even if not all the obligations of the treaty are eventually implemented), we identified a sub-type of issue-specific engagement. Issue-specific engagement occurs when political authorities decide to engage with only one or some obligations of the treaty. In this type of engagement, they do not engage with the treaty 'as a whole', in a comprehensive way, but limit their engagement to a specific issue. This type of engagement can be a first step leading to a more comprehensive implementation-centred engagement or, to the contrary, can follow an implementation-centred engagement by dealing

---

[23] See footnote 12.

with a specific issue that would not have been dealt with before. We observed some cases in which a law reformed adapted the existing legislation to consider a specific issue raised by a treaty. For example, the modification of the Protection against Violence Act (*Gewaltschutzgesetz*) in Zurich to extend the scope of application so as to help victims of stalking. This reform notably referred to the obligation made by the Istanbul Convention to punish stalking (art. 34, IC). Hereafter, we present a paradigmatic case that directly aims at implementing one specific article of the CRPD by modifying the cantonal constitution.

In the canton of Geneva, a parliamentary commission studied a draft constitutional law on the political rights of persons with disabilities. The CRPD played no role whatsoever at the beginning of this process. Rather, the authorities' original idea was to simply align the cantonal constitutional text with the federal legislation to address the practical problem of having to deal with different electoral registers at the cantonal and the federal level.[24] The CRPD (nor the European Convention on Human Right) appears nowhere in the report of the government presenting the new law.[25] During the commission's work, cantonal MPs decided to seek input from two professors of constitutional law from the University of Geneva who brought the attention of the commission to the fact that Switzerland was a party to the CRPD and that the treaty was relevant for the canton.[26] The commission then invited Caroline Hess-Klein, an expert in disability law and a representative of the CSO *Inclusion Handicap*.

It was only through these hearings that the parliamentary commission and the cantonal government realised that the draft constitutional law was not aligned with international law. Subsequently, cantonal MPs drafted their own attempt to modify the cantonal constitution. They not only mentioned the CRPD in the explanatory text, but entitled their proposal as a draft law to 'ensure conformity with the CRPD' more than a year later.[27] The commission of cantonal MPs proposed an amendment to ensure that no one with a disability would be denied political rights at the cantonal level. This amendment was ultimately transformed into a constitutional law reform entitled 'Constitutional Law Amending the Constitution of the Republic and Canton of Geneva (Implementation of Article 29 of the UN Convention on the Rights

---

[24] There are elections and referenda at municipal, cantonal and federal level, so if the rules on the denial of political rights differ between the various levels, this can create administrative and logistical challenges.

[25] Canton of Geneva, Draft law and explanations, PL 11969, p. 3, 14 September 2016, https://ge.ch/grandconseil/data/texte/PL11969.pdf.

[26] Three interviews with members of the cantonal parliament (from the Liberal-Radical Party, the Social Democratic Party and the far-left party 'Ensemble à Gauche') Geneva, 14 and 17 March, and 27 April 2022.

[27] Canton of Geneva, Draft law and explications, PL 12211, 3 November 2017, https://ge.ch/grandconseil/data/texte/PL12211.pdf.

of Persons with Disabilities—CRPD) (A 2 00 – 12211)'. On 29 November 2020, a large majority (74.77% of voters) accepted the reform.[28]

This example illustrates how subnational political authorities did not originally intend a reform to implement an obligation of the CRPD as such. Rather, this type of engagement occurred when the relevant subnational authorities tried to address a concrete issue and 'en route' discovered that they were drafting legislative modifications in a way that was not compatible with the CRPD and the authorities then started to look more closely into article 29 of the CRPD on political rights of persons with disabilities. It is worth noting the pivotal role played by the parliamentary commission, academic experts and a civil society representative, who effectively communicated to the parliamentarians about their international obligations and the evolving landscape of international law. By using the treaty as a legal basis, members of the commission drafted a motion engaging with the CRPD to implement Article 29 of the CRPD by modifying the cantonal constitution, eventually improving the political rights enjoyment of persons with disabilities at the subnational level.

This case serves as an example for other cantons who are studying the possibility of following Geneva and also improving the political rights of persons with disabilities in their canton.

We will now turn to the second type of implementation-centred engagement: this time, the route is not a legislative action, but action plans crafted within the cantonal administration.

5.2.1.3 The Bureaucratic Way: Adopting Action Plans

Subnational political authorities can also carry out an implementation-centred engagement with a treaty by adopting an action plan aimed at implementing a human rights treaty. The development of an action plan involves specialised policy bureaucrats who are tasked to implement the treaty or managing the policy area related to the treaty. The goal of such an instrument is to (re)organise the actions, means, funding, instruments, actors, institutional framework and sometimes the goals and policy paradigm (cognitive dimension) in the domain targeted by the treaty. An action plan is about co-ordinating and organising public policy, so we consider it a policy bureaucratic approach (Page & Jenkins, 2005) to implementation-centred engagement. The measures contained in an action plan do not always require parliamentary ratification, but the support of the cantonal government is necessary for practical and financial reasons.

We observed that the adoption of action plans is a particularly popular type of implementation-centred engagement in relation to the Istanbul Convention.

---

[28] Loi constitutionnelle modifiant la constitution de la République et canton de Genève (Cst-GE) (Mise en oeuvre e l'article 29 de la Convention de l'ONU relative aux droits des personnes handicapées—CDPH) (A 200–12211), du 27 février 2020), adopted in a popular referendum: https://www.ge.ch/votations/20201129/cantonal/.

According to a 2023 stocktaking report of the Swiss Conference against Domestic Violence (CSVD), 20 cantons have already adopted cantonal action plans or series of measures mandated by the cantonal government to fight against violence against women and/or domestic violence, with a view to implement the Istanbul Convention. According to our interviewees, action plans have been encouraged by the Swiss Conference against Domestic Violence and the Federal Office for Gender Equality. Most specialised policy bureaucrats whom we interviewed explained that they used the report of the Swiss Conference against Domestic Violence and the seven priority themes to build their stocktaking report, and then their action plan. Thus, they use mediations (Miaz, 2019) and implementation mechanisms (Kaempfer, 2021) to interpret the treaty and relate it to local realities. The report of the Swiss Conference against Domestic Violence thus significantly shapes the ways political authorities at the subnational level engage with the treaty. Specialised policy bureaucrats elaborating action plans refer not only (and even sometimes not at all) to the human rights treaty as such, but also (or only) to the report of the Swiss Conference against Domestic Violence. We qualify this type of engagement as implementation-centred as there is a commitment by the subnational political authorities to deal with the treaty, including when the authorities only refer to the report prepared at the inter-cantonal level.

Elaborating action plans suggests a back-and-forth process between treaty and field needs. The process of developing action plans, much like the process of elaborating law reforms, often involves a collaboration between policy bureaucrats, street-level organisations and civil society groups. For all the action plans identified in this study, the specialised policy bureaucrats are the key actors co-ordinating the elaboration of the action plan. Typically, members of cantonal parliaments do not play a significant role in this process, but we observed that they play an important role earlier in the process when they use the treaty to push the cantonal government to engage with it by elaborating an action plan (see Chapter 4 on the example from Zurich in relation to the Istanbul Convention, where use of the treaty by individual parliamentarians was decisive to spur a later engagement by the subnational authorities). In Vaud, a specialised policy bureaucrat explained that following the adoption of the cantonal 'Law on the Organisation of the Fight against Domestic Violence' in 2017,[29] the Federal Office for Gender Equality collaborated with the cantonal commission on the fight against domestic violence to develop an action plan. This commission was composed of various bureaucratic services, such as the Welfare and Social Assistance Department, the Youth Protection Service, the cantonal police, the judiciary, and institutions specialising in the treatment of domestic violence, including housing and victim support services.

---

[29] Canton of Vaud, Loi d'organisation de la prévention et de la lutte contre la violence domestique, 26 September 2017, https://prestations.vd.ch/pub/blv-publication/actes/consolide/211.12?key=1678646562856&id=0d5932f8-2b0d-478d-83ec-f68a77e943a1.

When subnational authorities engage with the treaty by initiating the establishment of a cantonal action plan, the cantonal administration considers different types of information. First, those elaborating on the action plan recounted that they aimed to respond to the needs and realities of the field. The engagement with the treaty thus implies a variety of actors working 'on the ground' to ensure that the action plan is in line with the context-specific needs of the field and the drafters engage in a collective and relational work. Second, in this process, the treaty is used alongside various documents and mediations. The specialised policy bureaucrat responsible for developing the action plan in Vaud explained that she relied not only on the Istanbul Convention, but also on the questionnaire sent by the GREVIO and the documentation provided by the Federal Office for Gender Equality. As a result, the action plans we identified in relation to the Istanbul Convention usually emphasise the seven priority themes identified by the Swiss Conference against Domestic Violence, the CSVD (on the role of the report by the CSVD, see Chapter 3) For instance, in the canton of Valais, the action plan follows these priority themes. It sets nine axes of intervention for the canton, based on both the report of the Swiss Conference against Domestic Violence and the recommendations made in a report that took stock of the existing measures in the canton:

> In short, we took these recommendations [of the report of the CSVD] along with the recommendations of the report [established by an external expert who works in an institution for victims of domestic violence in another canton] and that's really what made up the architecture of our action plan, and for us it was important that the action plan be validated afterwards by the cantonal government, and then that's really our roadmap.[30]

Similarly, the subnational government in the canton of Zurich adopted an action plan that draws heavily from the recommendations of the CSVD. The authorities decided to engage comprehensively with the Istanbul Convention as a result of uses of the treaty by two cantonal MPs (see Chapter 4) and tasked their bureaucracy to elaborate an action plan. The administration used, 'above all' the report of the Swiss Conference against Domestic Violence.[31] The cantonal government approved the final list of measures on 31 March 2021[32] and each of the 16 measures references specific articles of the Istanbul

---

[30] Interview with the Head of the Co-ordinating Office for Disability Issues, Social Action Department, Valais, 23 March 2022.

[31] Interview with the two Co-directors of the Domestic Violence Intervention Centre, Zurich, 23 April 2021.

[32] Canton of Zurich, Decision of the cantonal government 'Violence against women, implementation of the Istanbul Convention in the Canton of Zurich; measures and establishment plan' (Decision 'Gewalt gegen Frauen, Umsetzung der Istanbul-Konvention im Kanton Zürich; Massnahmen und Stellenplan'), Extract from the minutes of the Government Council of the Canton of Zurich, Meeting of

Convention. The decision also includes an additional full-time position and a stronger Intervention Centre against Domestic Violence.

Just like the 'in chain' reaction observed after the adoption of a law on the rights of persons with disabilities in the canton of Basel-Stadt, we also observe a mechanism of diffusion in which specialised policy bureaucrats draw inspiration from examples set by other cantons. For instance, in the small canton of Jura, a specialised policy bureaucrat explains that she followed the lead of the canton of Valais, which had previously adopted an action plan.[33] Therefore, this engagement pattern is also disseminated through examples of 'good practices' inspiring other cantons.

In summary, action plans typically start by taking stock of the existing measures and identifying the gaps and needs on the ground. They involve specialised policy bureaucrats, other public sector organisations, street-level actors, civil society organisations and non-profit organisations involved in public policy. In the case of the CRPD, persons concerned have also been involved through consultative commissions and some cantonal authorities initiated the elaboration of an action plan. The subnational government in Zurich adopted such an action plan for the CRPD and another one is being prepared in Neuchâtel. Compared to the Istanbul Convention, however, implementation-centred engagement by way of adopting an action plan seems less common.

5.2.1.4 The Continuation of Implementation-Centred Engagement After Legislative Change or the Adoption of an Action Plan

So far, we have distinguished two sub-types of implementation-centred engagement: one going through the cantonal parliament and the other one based on action plans elaborated by the specialised bureaucracy. What remains to be mentioned in this section is the combination of the two within one and the same cantonal jurisdiction and the progressive and intertwined processes. Implementation-centred engagement with a treaty does not end with the adoption of a law or an action plan. Rather, it is a progressive and continuous process, as seen in Neuchâtel, where after the adoption of the law on domestic violence in 2019, cantonal MPs used various parliamentary tools to ask questions about specific issues related to the Istanbul Convention. In response, in June 2022, the cantonal government presented an information report on the 'Cantonal action plan for the prevention and fight against domestic violence'.[34] This example illustrates that the implementation-centred engagement with a treaty is an ongoing process that continues as the treaty

---

31 March 2021, https://www.zh.ch/bin/zhweb/publish/regierungsratsbeschluss-unterlagen./2021/338/RRB-2021-0338.pdf.

[33] Interview 61 with a Head of Domain, Social Action Department, Jura, 6 April 2022. *Translated from French.*

[34] Canton of Neuchâtel, Plan d'action neuchâtelois de prévention et de lutte contre la violence domestique, June 2022, https://www.ne.ch/autorites/DECS/OPFE/violence-conjugale/Documents/Plan%20d%27action%20violence%20domestique_I.pdf.

becomes part of the legal landscape and public policy. Specialised policy bureaucrats, parliamentarians and civil society can all drive law reforms, and while specialised policy bureaucrats are the key actors in action plans, members of cantonal parliaments can play a supporting or agenda-setting role. In other words, the subnational authorities' engagement leads to further uses of the treaty by subnational actors and those uses, in turn, again stimulate further engagement by the authorities.

Ultimately, the implementation-centred engagements examined in this section have a common goal of implementing a treaty's obligations and we can say with reasonable confidence that such engagement is an ideal starting point for a dynamic implementation process that promises to lead to practical improvements of human rights realisation in real-life situations.

Not surprisingly, however, not all subnational political authorities opt for what we have termed implementation-centred engagement. We will now turn to what we call initiating engagement.

5.2.2 Initiating Engagement

We observed initiating engagement in certain cantons where there are limited or no previous policy measures in the domain covered by the relevant treaty. Initiating engagement represents a crucial first step towards implementing at least some aspects of the treaty. Typically, an initiating engagement originates with cantonal bureaucracies, who request the establishment of an office or allocation of additional resources. In this context, the treaty is leveraged as a cognitive, legal and political resource by bureaucrats to institutionalise and co-ordinate policymaking in the relevant domain. Contrary to implementation-centred engagement, the treaty is not used as a starting point for legislative changes or an action plan with a view to implement the treaty as such, but initiating engagement aims at the allocation of some resources and mandates to take stock of the situation and suggest improvements.

We have observed such a pattern of initiating engagement with the Istanbul Convention in Schaffhausen. In this small canton (82,537 inhabitants in 2021), the head of the Social Security Office was, among many other tasks, also responsible for addressing issues related to domestic violence, and viewed the Istanbul Convention as a significant opportunity to secure resources, including a new position dedicated to implementing the Istanbul Convention:

> So for us, the Istanbul Convention is a huge opportunity. It is the best legitimisation in this field, the need to act, to comply; to do more in qualitative and quantitative terms than we have done so far. This is a huge opportunity. I believe that if we did not have this Istanbul Convention, it would have been much more difficult to politically legitimise doing more in this area.[35]

---

[35] Interview with a Head of Service, Social Welfare Office, Schaffhausen, 19 May 2021.

During our discussions, the interviewee explained that there was no comprehensive strategy in place to prevent and combat violence against women and domestic violence, and that he thought the domain lacked co-ordination. The initiating engagement by the public authorities led to the creation of a new position: the Co-ordination Office for the Prevention of Violence against Women and Domestic Violence. Its primary task is to identify gaps in this area and work towards addressing them.

> We knew that there were gaps, but we had neither the resources nor the mandate to identify these gaps. But we knew that, for example, in the area of perpetrator prevention, also in dealing with children in victim assistance, etc., there are various gaps […].[36]

The establishment of this new office has facilitated the institutionalisation and organisation of co-ordination efforts within this policy domain.

> The position is the Co-ordination Office for the Prevention of Violence against Women and Domestic Violence Istanbul Convention. So it's really clear: we are the co-ordinating body for the implementation of the Istanbul Convention. […] And there is a clear mandate from the government council for this position. So then to the question, what are your frameworks and requests, and [what my tasks are]. First and foremost, that is really to co-ordinate the actors, to drive the implementation of the Convention and immediately, to promote this interdisciplinary cooperation.[37]

To summarise this example, a bureaucrat's use of the treaty succeeded in securing at least an initiating engagement with the Istanbul Convention. The impetus for action first came from the Social Affairs Office, which then led to the establishment of the Co-ordination Office. The cantonal government supported the proposal to create a new position, and the cantonal parliament approved the proposition,[38] resulting in the creation of the Co-ordination Office.[39] Compared to implementation-centred engagement, the engagement of the subnational political authorities is much more limited: there is no overarching commitment (yet) to implement the relevant treaty as such, but

---

[36] Ibid.

[37] Interview with the Head of the Co-ordination Office for the Prevention of Violence against Women and Domestic Violence (Istanbul Convention), Schaffhausen, 8 February 2021.

[38] Minutes of the 17th Session, Cantonal Parliament of Schaffhausen, 18 November 2019, 934–947.

[39] Jurga Wüger, 'Bei mir laufen alle Fäden zusammen', *Schaffhauser Nachrichten*, 25 November 2020, https://www.shn.ch/region/kanton/2020-11-25/bei-mir-laufen-alle-faeden-zusammen.

a willingness to initiate a certain institutionalisation and the provision of additional resources to address at least some aspects of the treaty. This initiating engagement was finally followed by a more implementation-centred one through the elaboration and adoption of the cantonal action plan 2022–2026 for the implementation of the Istanbul Convention.

Another initiating engagement also involved a commitment to undertake a preliminary stocktaking exercise and the creation of a new position within the cantonal administration. In the small canton of Glarus (40,370 inhabitants in 2021), a parliamentary intervention by the members of the Social Democratic Party on the Istanbul Convention asked for information about the departments responsible for the issue of violence against women and domestic violence and the implementation of the measures planned by the Convention.[40] This interpellation was a starting point that led the cantonal bureaucracy to take stock of what exists in the canton and to identify the gaps, based on the report of the Swiss Conference against Domestic Violence.

> It was the point where we knew: oh, now we really have to deal with it. I think the [Social Democratic Party] has already hit a nerve to say 'hey, there is this Convention, where does the canton of Glarus stand'. And that was really the first moment – to be honest – where I think the canton seriously dealt with this Istanbul Convention. And we had to do like a stocktaking: where do we stand, what do we already have, where do we still have to go? And on the basis of this interpellation – which was then also answered to the satisfaction of the Social Democratic Party – we naturally then thought about it internally and knew clearly that we do not yet fulfil some points, we need such a co-ordination office. We need a guardian of this Convention, because otherwise in the day-to-day business, yes, it gets lost. And now we are at this point where we can clearly say: yes, the engagement is there, now we create this office or designate this office and equip it sufficiently.[41]

In the bureaucracy, the Head of Social Services[42] is responsible the prevention and fight of violence against women and domestic violence, but without any resources to fulfil this task. Consequently, the Head of Social Services sought additional resources, especially the creation of a new position (50%) in her office to 'really implement the Istanbul Convention'.[43] Finally, in February 2022, the cantonal government established the domestic violence unit. The responsibilities of this specialised office for domestic violence were defined by a working group that included the Social Services, victim assistance and counselling, and the cantonal police. The unit's duties are to promote the

---

[40] Interpellation 'Istanbul Convention', filed by Sarah Küng Hefti and Christian Büttiker (SP), Cantonal Parliament, Glarus, 6 December 2018.

[41] Interview with the Head of Social Services, Glarus, 4 March 2021.

[42] Contrary to other cantons, social services are cantonal tasks (not municipal ones).

[43] Interview with the Head of Social Services, Glarus, 4 March 2021.

implementation of the Istanbul Convention and to co-ordinate efforts within the agencies involved.[44]

We observed a gradual evolution of the subnational political authorities' engagement with the Istanbul Convention: from a modest initiating engagement, it is possible that the authorities begin to move towards a more implementation-centred engagement, strengthening over time the commitment not 'only' to take stock and provide some resources, but to conceive that the treaty as such must be implemented. In both examples of initiating engagement presented here, the human rights treaties served as a catalyst for the policy process, resulting in the establishment, institutionalisation and restructuring of the policy domain. These initial steps can pave the way for further engagement with the treaties, such as the development of an action plan or the creation of a new law. Therefore, we refer to these measures as initiating engagement.

In addition to implementation-centred and initiating engagement, a third type of engagement is embedded engagement.

5.2.3 Embedded Engagement

Embedded engagement with a convention occurs when a treaty is used within a legislative project whose main goal is not the implementation of the treaty or compliance with it, nor is the treaty the starting point for the law reform or policy measures. The use of and reference to the treaty are part of the arguments, or even of the cognitive resources in the policy process, but they are not the main ones. Thus, the treaty—usually specific obligations of the treaty—is used as a legal argument among other legal references to justify the reform, which engages with the treaty only on specific obligations. Engagement with the treaty is thus embedded in a broader legislative project. This type of engagement can combine with an implementation-centred engagement.

In Geneva, for example, we observed different intertwined patterns of engagement with the Istanbul Convention, even one aiming at the implementation of the treaty through an action plan. Besides this implementation-centred engagement, we also observed an embedded engagement in the case of the draft law on equality and the fight against gender-based violence and discrimination filed in the cantonal parliament of Geneva on 16 December 2020 by the cantonal government. While the Istanbul Convention is one of several legal references, the draft law's aims do not centre on the Istanbul Convention. As the Head of the Cantonal Office for the Promotion of Equality and Prevention of Violence explained to us, she initiated work on this draft law even before Switzerland ratified the Istanbul Convention:

---

[44] Canton Glarus, 'Kanton Glarus baut Fachstelle häusliche Gewalt auf', *Public Newsroom*, https://www.gl.ch/public-newsroom.html/31/newsroomnews/2153/prin, 15 February 2022.

We have an equality law which is, which has been elaborated, which is in consultation now, equality and fight against gender violence, so that's at the Geneva cantonal level, that too was not linked to the Istanbul Convention, we had started that quite a while ago.[45]

The drafters of the law did engage with the Istanbul Convention. For instance, on the issue of sexual harassment, the draft law mentions the Istanbul Convention.[46] The IC is also used to provide education in line with the treaty's goal to prevent sexism. Here, the weight given to the Istanbul Convention is not particularly high, probably because the canton of Geneva, compared to many other cantons, already had an elaborate legislative and institutional framework. In this case, the engagement with the treaty happens 'on the go', as a welcome additional layer of arguments.

The example above constitutes an embedded engagement with the treaty, as the engagement with specific obligations of the treaty is embedded in this broader, related law project that did not directly aim at addressing the implementation of the treaty. It is worth noting that such embedded engagement may occur in parallel to an implementation-centred engagement with the treaty, where the canton may have taken other measures to implement the human rights treaty.

5.2.4 *Synthesis: Types of Engagement with International Treaties*

To conclude this section, we identified different types of engagement that we classified through the goals of the process, the types of measures taken and the trajectories of the process. We showed that several types of engagement aim at implementing the treaty or at preparing the implementation of the treaty (implementation-centred and initiating engagement). Besides, we also identified embedded engagement, through which the subnational authorities use a treaty or specific obligations contained therein when they are pursuing a concrete objective during an already ongoing process for which the implementation of the treaty is not the starting point, nor the goal of the project.

Implementation-centred engagement includes enacting laws or making reforms to clarify the issue in question, establish new rights, and provide a solid legal basis for a new policy framework. The process also involves developing and implementing action plans in line with the new policy, ultimately reorganising the entire policy field and its measures. Implementation-centred engagement is a crucial step in the empirical life of a treaty at the subnational level and denotes a shift where decisions are often made which will ultimately lead to better rights implementation.

---

[45] Interview with the Head of the Cantonal Office for the Promotion of Equality and Prevention of Violence, Geneva, 1 July 2020.

[46] 'Draft law on equality and the fight against gender-based violence and discrimination' (*title translated from French*), PL 12843, 16 December 2020, p. 30.

In cantons where there were only a few concrete and unified public policies in the domain covered by the treaty, initiating engagement can lead to institutionalisation and the impetus of a new public policy. This engagement results in the creation of new bureaucratic positions, new offices specialised in the issue covered by the treaty, and new means to implement the treaty. Thus, the initiating engagement mainly involves new actors and a new institutional framework, which can, as we saw for the canton of Schaffhausen, open the space for a more implementation-centred engagement involving new instruments, a new institutional framework and cognitive changes in public policy.

Finally, embedded engagement often occurs when an engagement with the treaty is included, embedded in a broader legislative project which does not directly aim at implementing the treaty of specific obligations. The embedded engagement is a pragmatic one as the broader law project provides an opportunity to engage (further) with the obligations of the treaty and, at the same time, to legally argue in favour of the legislative project. We expect to increasingly observe this type of engagement as the treaties become part of the common legal landscape of cantonal authorities and as the latter increasingly develop implementation-centred engagement. In doing so, we expect that they will become interested in pursuing treaty-related issues that will lead them to continue to engage with some of the treaty's obligations by developing public policies in related areas that touch certain aspects of the treaty.

5.3 Comparative Outlook and Conditions for Engagement

This section offers a comparative outlook to distil similarities and differences in how uses translate into engagement and the different patterns of engagement with the two treaties serving as case studies, and we discuss the conditions shaping the turn from uses to engagement and the engagement patterns.

We begin by reflecting on the uses that did not lead to engagement in order to identify limiting factors.

5.3.1 From Uses to Engagement? Factors Limiting Subnational Engagement

In this section, we present cases where subnational actors, such as specialised policy bureaucrats, experts and members of cantonal parliaments, have used the treaty pushing for policy measures, but where political authorities have then declined to take action or simply did not react, i.e. there was *no engagement*. We classify these uses according to the conditions hindering the engagement with the treaty, and we discuss these conditions. These include the weakness of left-wing political parties in the cantonal parliament and government, an underdeveloped existing policy—an engagement with the treaty implying a significant policy change—a perception of weak financial resources (or potential to increase them) or weak cantonal policy investments, and no specialised bureaucracy. Small cantons tend to be more likely to find themselves in such situations.

Chapter 4 has shown that subnational actors often use treaties with the aim of pushing political authorities to take policy measures (action plans, laws and public policies). When this happens as a result of the treaty, we stated that political authorities engage with the treaty. However, the turn from uses to engagement does not always occur. In certain cantons, we observed that even where there are parliamentary interventions calling for the implementation of the Istanbul Convention or the CRPD respectively, the political authorities do not engage with the treaty and do not take concrete measures. For example, in the case of the Istanbul Convention, several cantons have not adopted specific measures to implement the treaty,[47] and the same observation is made for the CRPD—probably at an even larger scale—as there are only a small minority of cantons that have adopted laws on inclusion, on the rights of persons with disabilities, and/or on self-determination. We can distinguish two main groups of limiting factors: an unfavourable political context and a real or perceived lack of resources.

5.3.1.1 Lack of Political Will or Unfavourable Political Balance of Power

How can we understand the occurrence of uses not leading to engagement? Several interviewees believe that the main reason for a lack of engagement relates to a 'lack of political will', which in turn, according to the interviewees, correlates with the political balance of power in cantonal parliaments and governments.

In Chapter 4, we observed that many uses came from left-wing cantonal MPs, all the more so if they have already been active in relation to issues related to gender equality, or human rights of persons with disabilities. Likewise, we observe that conservative parliaments and/or governments, i.e. a low presence of left-wing politicians, may limit or hinder the engagement with a treaty.

Several interviewees referred to a 'lack of political will' to explain the lack of engagement by subnational authorities with regard to the examined international human rights treaties. This was obvious in at least three interviews with members of administrations who lamented the 'lack of political will' to give them adequate resources to act in this area. This 'political will' refers to political feasibility conditions that are in turn related to the political profile and

---

[47] Interview 14 with the Head of the Cantonal Office for the Promotion of Equality and Prevention of Violence, Geneva, 1 July 2020.

Swiss Conference on Domestic Violence, 'Mise en œuvre de la Convention d'Istanbul au niveau des cantons. Etats des lieux et mesures à entreprendre' (Appendix 1), September 2018, www.csvd.ch in: Réseau Convention d'Istanbul (eds), «Mise en œuvre de la Convention d'Istanbul en Suisse. Rapport alternatif de la société civile», June 2021, https://istanbulkonvention.ch/assets/images/elements/Rapport_alternatif_Reseau_Convention_Istanbul.pdf.

partisan affiliation of the ministers in charge of these files in these cantons. A head of department of an Office for Social Affairs in a canton where no action has been taken as a result of the Istanbul Convention explained that gender equality and violence against women were not considered a priority on the political agenda.[48] According to another interviewee, the attitude of the cantonal government and the weight of political conservatism in the cantonal government and parliament limit the possibilities for members of the administrations to propose political or legal measures, as well as additional financial or human resources.[49]

One of the cantons in which we conducted our interviews falls into this category of cantons where, despite parliamentary interpellations in favour of the implementation of the Istanbul Convention, a political majority in the government and parliament—according to our interviewees—do not consider it a priority, or even a 'political topic' in the canton. This is a rather small conservative canton with a right-wing majority in the cantonal parliament and government and with the right-wing Swiss People's Party as the largest political party. As one of our interviewees puts it, the issues of domestic violence or violence against women are topics that 'are hardly ever discussed in the cantonal government or parliament'.[50] A staff member of a cantonal service against domestic violence explains that nobody at the cantonal roundtable on domestic violence has ever heard of the Istanbul Convention or of the CEDAW.[51]

In this canton, two cantonal MPs from the Social Democratic Party relayed the parliamentary interpellation but removed a question on transgender persons, considering that the inclusion of a reference to transgender persons would have been counterproductive given the conservative context of the canton. The goal was to concentrate on domestic violence and at least discuss the Istanbul Convention.[52] This interpellation made it possible to obtain an inventory from the cantonal government regarding the measures and infrastructures to fight violence against women and domestic violence but did not lead to an engagement by the political authorities with the Istanbul Convention. An interviewee confirmed that for the cantonal political authorities, the implementation of the Istanbul Convention 'is not on the agenda, it is not planned'.[53]

Thus, the ability to use the Istanbul Convention as a political, legal, cognitive or practical resource to achieve the engagement of the relevant subnational

---

[48] Interview with a Head of Service, May 2021. (For confidentiality issues we choose to anonymise this interview and the ones in the following footnotes).

[49] Interview with a Head of Office, April 2021.

[50] Interview with a specialised bureaucrat, December 2020.

[51] Interview with a specialised bureaucrat, January 2021.

[52] Interview with a cantonal MP from the Social Democratic Party in this small canton, 28 January 2021.

[53] Interview with X, Canton Y, 2021.

political authorities, as well as a window of opportunity, depends not only on civil servants or parliamentarians, but also on the cantonal political context, which shapes the possibilities of seizing the treaty and taking political or legal measures in this area. In the most conservative cantons, a balance of power in favour of the conservative right in the cantonal government and parliament limits the possibilities for legal and political changes related to the Istanbul Convention. Specialised policy bureaucrats, as they anticipate the reactions of their cantonal government and the parliament, cannot use the Istanbul Convention as a resource in the same way according to the cantonal context and balance of power.

5.3.1.2 Lack of Financial Resources
Financial constraints and priorities and the economic context of the canton can also hinder the engagement of subnational political authorities with a treaty. Catherine Le Bris and Pierre-Edouard Weill also explain, on the French case, that local policies to implement human rights heavily depend on the financial and institutional resources of local authorities (Le Bris & Weill, 2022). In small cantons in particular, there is a discourse—and sometimes a political strategy—about the lack of availability of financial resources to invest in new 'costly' policy measures, all the more so when the economic context is 'complicated'. Swiss cantons are sovereign in tax matters but increasing the availability of resources or setting priorities differently is of course politically sensitive. One civil servant explained that 'change must come from above' because, while the 'large' cantons such as Berne, Zurich, Geneva or Vaud have working groups for the implementation of the Istanbul Convention, smaller cantons have 'small' administrations with much more limited means 'and we can hardly cope with this additional burden'. According to her, it is therefore necessary to go 'beyond international law' by making federal laws that will encourage subnational political authorities like the ones in her canton to engage with the treaty and budget the necessary resources for its implementation.[54]

5.3.2 Enabling Conditions: Alignment with Pre-Existing Policies and Strong Specialised Policy Bureaucracy

Effective engagement with human rights treaties requires a comprehensive approach tailored to the specific policy domain. When public policy in cantons aligns, at least to some extent, with the treaty's approach, engagement with the treaty reinforces and legitimises existing efforts and measures. For example, in certain cantons, especially the French-speaking ones, the fight against domestic violence and violence against women more broadly was already moving in the same direction as the Istanbul Convention. In these cases, ratification of the Istanbul Convention offered an opportunity to enhance existing measures with innovative means and a new dynamic. At the federal level, the authorities

[54] Ibid.

adopted an action plan to continue the momentum initiated by the Istanbul Convention. Meanwhile, at the cantonal level, subnational political authorities took measures like the creation of new positions, law reforms, and action plans to engage with the treaty. Federal and inter-cantonal actors supported these processes by playing a critical role in promoting subnational engagement through reports, recommendations, and a national action plan encouraging cantons to take measures, providing them with 'good practices' and priorities, and highlighting a federal 'political will'. Overall, specialised policy bureaucrats were primarily involved in this bureaucratic approach, with parliamentarians playing a smaller role.

Conversely, engaging with the Convention on the Rights of Persons with Disabilities (CRPD) at the cantonal level proved to be more challenging. One major obstacle was the significant paradigm shift (Heyer, 2015) required by the CRPD compared to existing cantonal disability policies. The CRPD emphasises autonomy, self-determination, and inclusion, which differ greatly from most cantonal policies. Therefore, implementing the CRPD requires changes across various sectors of the administration and public policy domains. Furthermore, the Federal Bureau for the Equality of People with Disabilities has fewer resources than the Federal Office for Gender Equality, limiting its capacity to lead or encourage the implementation of the CRPD in the cantons. Despite these challenges, several subnational political authorities have taken steps to engage with the CRPD. Prioritising the revision or adoption of laws over other measures, such as creating action plans and establishing new positions, highlights an approach that seems to more heavily prioritise legislative measures than what we found for the Istanbul Convention. This may be due to disability policy administrations relying on legal experts in their policy processes, or a higher need of legislative changes to ensure the implementation of the treaty obligations. The measures taken promote inclusion, self-determination, and the rights of persons with disabilities in the concerned cantons, constituting an engagement with the treaty. They offer an opportunity to take a new policy path that can have a long-term impact on improving the inclusion of persons with disabilities.

Table 5.1 presents the different types of engagement we identified and summarises the various goals pursued by the policy process, the measures taken, dimensions of policy change, trajectories, and the conditions we identify as favourable to that type of engagement. Lastly, the table indicates in which canton we observed a given type of engagement.

5.4 Conclusion

This chapter presented an overview of the three categories of engagement that we observed in our case studies on the Istanbul Convention and the CRPD. We observed different patterns of engagement depending on various factors and conditions specific to the cantons where the subnational authorities engage with human rights treaties. Specifically, when a public policy in the

Table 5.1 Different types of engagement with human rights treaties

Types of engagement	Goals	Types of measures	Trajectories	Conditions	Cases
Implementation-centred Engagement Sub-type: Issue-specific engagement	Implementing the treaty 'as a whole' Or one or specific obligations of the treaty (issue-specific engagement)	• New law • Law reform • Constitutional reform • Action plan • Specific policy measures • Additional resources	*Starting point*: Parliamentary intervention OR cantonal bureaucracy *Policymaking process*: Action plan or law project made by bureaucracy (and ad hoc commission) • Government approval (if an action plan, it is enforced), *If law or financial resources to be approved*: • Parliamentary commission • Parliament votes OR Law reform proposed by members of parliament (e.g. parliamentary commission) or if popular or parliamentary initiative • Parliamentary commission • Parliament votes If constitutional reform: People vote (referendum)	Favouring conditions: • Strong left-wing • Specialised bureaucracy • Financial resources • Already-existing policy Hindering conditions: • Small canton	IC: GE, NE, ZH, BE, VS, JU CRDP: NE, VS, FR, BS, BL, ZH, BE, GE, SH

Types of engagement	Goals	Types of measures	Trajectories	Conditions	Cases
Initiating engagement	Getting resources to prepare the implementation of the treaty	• Creation of bureaucratic position to implement the treaty • Additional resources • Action plan	*Starting point*: Parliamentary intervention OR cantonal bureaucracy (through information) *Policymaking process*: Bureaucracy's proposals • Government approves • Parliament debates and votes	Favouring conditions: • Balance of power with left-wing in parliament and/or government • Presence of left-wing cantonal MP or MCG • Financial resources	IC: SH, GL
Embedded engagement	The implementation of specific obligation may not be the main goal of the policy change, but the treaty is used as a legal argument supporting the policy change (or specific measure included in the proposal). Even if the aim is not directly to implement the treaty, specific obligations are used as a legal and/or cognitive resource and reference to support the project or specific measures	• New law or law reform or policy measures (an engagement with specific obligations of the treaty is included in the project to support it 'as a whole' or to justify specific legal articles or policy proposals)	Use of the treaty as an argument to take measures or to go further in a related (but different) policy domain or issue (can be additional or parallel to the implementation-centred engagement)	Favouring conditions: • Strong left-wing • Specialised bureaucracy • Financial resources • Already-existing policy (particularly important) Hindering conditions: • Small canton	IC: GE

For a list of the acronyms, see https://www.bfs.admin.ch/bfs/en/home/basics/symbolsabbreviations.html#accordion1714280292791 domain and direction of a treaty is already well-established in a given canton, the possibility that uses of the treaty lead to implementation-centred engagement is higher than when a canton has no pre-existing policy. Conversely, in cantons that are less receptive to implementation-centred engagement, uses are more likely to lead to a more modest, initiating engagement, which could involve the creation of a new position within the cantonal administration.

This chapter also highlighted that engaging with the Istanbul Convention was encouraged by federal and inter-cantonal authorities and was facilitated by existing policies—conducted by specialised policy bureaucracies—to combat domestic violence[55] in several cantons, resulting in an effective bureaucratic approach through the adoption of action plans. Conversely, engagement with the CRPD proved to be more challenging due to the substantial paradigm shifts required in cantonal policies regarding disability, often first requiring awareness-raising, legal analysis, and input from academic experts. In all cases, engaging with the treaty has contributed to the implementation in one way or another. As we cautioned in the introductory chapter, engagement is no guarantee for successful or complete implementation, let alone compliance. But this chapter illustrated how engagement is a key phenomenon if we are to understand the various steps that follow when subnational political authorities commit to deal with a treaty.

In the sixth and final chapter of this book, we take a step back, synthesise the results and reflect on what is next in terms of future research.

REFERENCES

Barnes, C. (2019). Understanding the Social Model of Disability: Past, Present and Future. In N. Watson, A. Rouldstone, & C. Thomas (Eds.), *Routledge Handbook of Disability Studies* (pp. 14–31). Routledge.

Donald, A., & Speck, A.-K. (2020). The Dynamics of Domestic Human Rights Implementation: Lessons from Qualitative Research in Europe. *Journal of Human Rights Practice*, *12*(1), 48–70. https://doi.org/10.1093/jhuman/huaa007

Dubois, V. (2012). The Fields of Public Policy. In M. Hilgers & E. Mangez (Eds.), *Social Field Theory: Concept and Applications* (pp. 199–220). Routledge.

Hess-Klein, C. (2017). Le cadre conventionnel et constitutionnel du droit de l'égalité des personnes handicapées. In F. Bellanger & T. Tanquerel (Eds.), *L'égalité des personnes handicapées: principes et concrétisation* (pp. 100). Schulthess Editions romandes.

Kaempfer, C. (2021). Domestic Mechanisms for the Implementation of International Obligations in the Swiss Cantons. *Swiss Review of International and European Law*, *31*(4), 541–563.

Haglund, L., & Stryker, R. (2015). *Closing the Rights Gap: From Human Rights to Social Transformation*. University of California Press.

---

[55] As mentioned before, however, domestic violence is only one part of the Istanbul Convention, which more broadly aims at preventing and combating *violence against women* and domestic violence.

Heyer, K. (2015). *Rights Enabled: The Disability Revolution, from the US, to Germany and Japan, to the United Nations*. University of Michigan Press.

Le Bris, C., & Weill, P.-E. (2022). Les élus locaux au défi de la protection des droits de l'homme: Entre « vœux pieux » et « lignes d'horizon ». *Droit et société, 2*(111), 401–421. https://doi.org/10.3917/drs1.111.0401

Miaz, J. (2019). Le Droit et ses médiations. Pratiques d'instruction des demandes d'asile et encadrement institutionnel des décisions. *Politique et Sociétés, 38*(1), 71–98.

Oliver, M. (2009). *Understanding Disability: From Theory to Practice* (2nd ed.). Palgrave Macmillan.

Page, E. C., & Jenkins, B. (2005). *Policy Bureaucracy*. Oxford University Press.

Risse, T., Ropp, S. C., & Sikkink, K. (1999). *The Power of Human Rights: International Norms and Domestic Change* (Vol. 66). Cambridge University Press.

Open Access This chapter is licensed under the terms of the Creative Commons Attribution 4.0 International License (http://creativecommons.org/licenses/by/4.0/), which permits use, sharing, adaptation, distribution and reproduction in any medium or format, as long as you give appropriate credit to the original author(s) and the source, provide a link to the Creative Commons license and indicate if changes were made.

The images or other third party material in this chapter are included in the chapter's Creative Commons license, unless indicated otherwise in a credit line to the material. If material is not included in the chapter's Creative Commons license and your intended use is not permitted by statutory regulation or exceeds the permitted use, you will need to obtain permission directly from the copyright holder.

CHAPTER 6

Towards a Contextualised Understanding of Human Rights Treaty Implementation

Abstract This chapter offers a synthesis of the arguments outlined in this book and discusses the main findings from the empirical study of the Swiss case. It appears that international law obligations do not impact the national level following a descending trajectory. Rather, they provide opportunities and constraints to a core group of subnational actors who use them to achieve their goals. These actors make the most of their agency and they can contribute to the engagement of political authorities with the treaties, ultimately enhancing local human rights protection. However, their contribution is specific and necessarily selective, and whether and how subnational political actors engage with human rights treaties is strongly shaped by favourable political conditions and institutional resources, whose absence is likely to undermine or at least strongly limit the process. Furthermore, in the last section of this chapter we sketch a new agenda for this area of research.

Keywords Human rights treaties · Implementation · Subnational actors · Uses of treaties

6.1 Taking Stock

The study of the way Swiss subnational political authorities engage with international human rights treaties suggests that obligations contained in a human rights treaty do not simply impose restrictions on the actions of subnational actors. Instead, a small group of specialised subnational actors interpret and actively use human rights treaties to achieve their goals. More specifically,

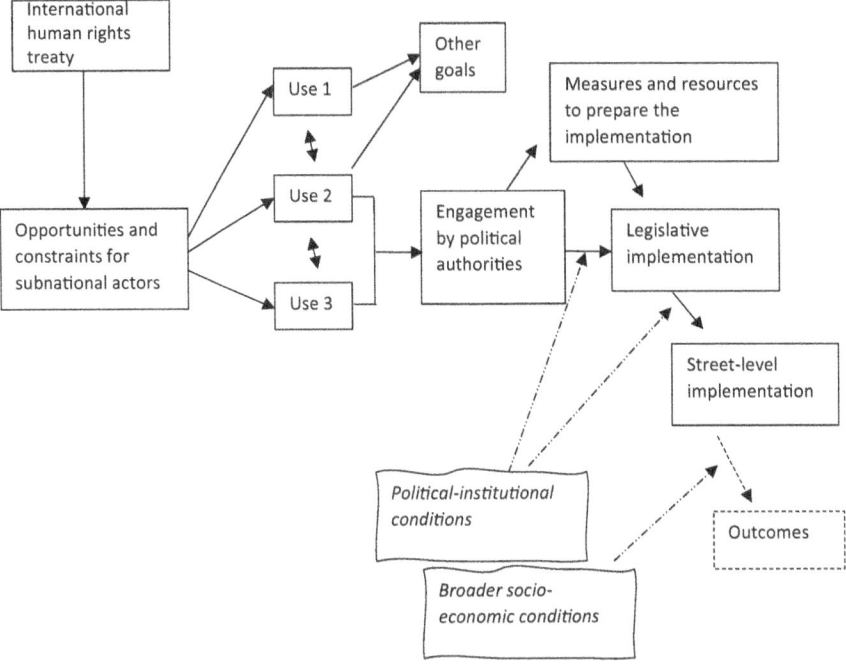

Fig. 6.1 Implementing international treaties

as outlined in the following two sections, our study has shown that subnational actors can use the treaties in various ways, consequently shaping how cantonal political authorities engage with them, in the view of ensuring their implementation (see Fig. 6.1).

6.1.1 Pre-ratification Phase and Implementation Strategies

Our study first revealed the importance of researching the pre-ratification procedure. Indeed, this procedure provides the national government with an opportunity to interpret the Convention, thus shaping the preferences of subnational units and orienting future implementation. We show that the government uses this procedure to put forward its narrative about the implications of ratification and thus convince domestic institutional actors, including subnational ones, to support ratification. Consequently, this procedure influences how political authorities will engage with the convention.

Post-ratification, we observe that implementation processes follow diverse patterns. In the case of the Council of Europe Convention on Preventing and Combating Violence against Women and Domestic Violence, better known as the Istanbul Convention, several state entities responsible for implementation designed implementation strategies, in what looks at first sight as a top-down process. For the the United Nations Convention on the Rights of Persons with Disabilities (CRPD Convention on the Rights of Persons with Disabilities (CRPD)), despite the establishment of a focal point responsible for implementation, we observe that there has been no explicit implementation strategy at the federal or inter-cantonal level. Then, academic experts stepped in and produced alternative tools to lead the implementation process. In any case, the mechanisms designed to elicit subnational engagement with the treaties are of a soft nature. They essentially correspond to information mechanisms, which seek to influence the behaviour of the subnational authorities through communication and advice. This enables the large leeway and the important role of subnational actors, who can use international treaties to achieve their goals, and often shape the engagement of subnational political authorities.

6.1.2 Uses

Our study has shown how subnational actors use human rights treaties to shape political agendas (Chapter 4; Jones & Baumgartner, 2005) at the cantonal level. Although treaties can be seen as constraints for subnational authorities, they also offer opportunities for actors to advance their interests. Specialised policy bureaucrats such as the director of the Equality Office in the public administration, the cantonal delegate for equality, or the head of the cantonal administration for support measures for people with disabilities have a prominent role therein. By making the most of their expert knowledge and connections with the international and federal level, they can use treaties to legitimise existing policies, gain resources, and reinforce their leading and co-ordinating position as focal points in policy processes. Subnational parliamentarians, i.e. members of cantonal parliaments, and especially those who are members of relevant parliamentary committees, can request the implementation of specific obligations and use treaties as legal and political arguments to support their claims, such as those related to equality, women's rights, and rights of persons with disabilities. Civil society actors can remind authorities of their legal obligations and can formulate and campaign around specific demands or suggest concrete implementation options. Academic experts can also, for instance, provide expertise on the interpretation of the obligations or on comparative examples in which certain options were tested.

As such, treaties offer important legal, political, and cognitive resources for subnational actors to set an issue on the agenda, frame a public problem, and impulse policy processes. Studying how actors refer to treaties suggests that the actors' uses are pragmatic and 'crafty' rather than predetermined by systematic legal analysis. As explained in Chapter 3, there is no linear implementation process to follow when it comes to implementing human rights treaties. Actors do not primarily consider treaty provisions as containing obligations to be fulfilled, but rather as a catalogue of opportunities to be selected according to their function and meaning they could acquire at the local level. Subnational actors can actively use these obligations by adapting them to the local context in accordance with their goals and interests. As such, international human rights treaties can provide a way to legitimise existing approaches or offer opportunities to reshape public policies in a given direction. Thereby, the processes through which international obligations are implemented at the subnational level are complex and iterative, involving both top-down and bottom-up dynamics. Implementing international human rights treaties is a continuous and incremental process that involves back-and-forth interactions and feedback loops, also entailing considerable room for manoeuvre of the involved actors. In that regard, it is nonetheless worth noting that not all actors are equal. As mentioned, specialised policy bureaucrats are particularly prominent at different stages in Swiss cantonal policy processes, with some standing out as key players—possessing the competencies, expertise, information, motivation and resources—who are able to exploit the opportunities provided by international human rights treaties and use them in accordance with their strategy. These actors are small in number but potentially very effective, factually working as policy entrepreneurs, whose mobilisation is fundamental in order to articulate policy ideas on the agenda of cantonal policy makers, open new windows of opportunity (Kingdon, 2014) and eventually trigger policy change (Mintrom & Norman, 2009). As we will see in the next section, the impact of these strategies is, however, highly dependent on the political context of the subnational unit at stake and the degree of favourableness of the political majority populating cantonal political institutions.

Contrariwise, the role of legislators is more marginal than what one could have expected, as members of cantonal parliaments are overall rather passive and, for the vast majority, they do not seem to make active use of international human rights treaties. This is not entirely surprising, as the literature has already pointed to the declining power of parliaments confronted to dominant executives, especially at the subnational level (Downs, 2014), whereby 'the initiative and control functions of parliaments are expected to be weak, with parliaments instead being confined to the role of ratifying bodies' (Benz & Papadopoulos, 2006, p. 3). It is also a Swiss peculiarity that semi-professional members of parliament are confronted with a more resourceful federal administration (Di Capua et al., 2022; Sciarini, 2015; Sciarini & Fischer, 2019) which in turn plays an increasingly important role in policy processes (Varone & Giauque, 2022). Furthermore, it is generally accepted that 'internationalization increases the role of governments vis-à-vis other domestic actors (i.e. parliament and interest groups) who do not have similar strategic resources' (Papadopoulos, 2008). This gap is even larger at the subnational level, where members of cantonal parliaments (cantonal MPs) are weakly professionalised and may be unaware of specific developments of international law: in most cantons, they spend less than 20% of a full-time equivalent on their parliamentary occupation (Eberli et al., 2019). And yet, the marginality of cantonal MPs is still puzzling and, in particular, potentially leading to political contestation. Even though specialised bureaucrats may have the best intentions, and indeed work for the greater good, they are less directly accountable to citizens than what parliamentarians would be, thus raising questions about the need for reinforcing the democratic legitimacy of these practices through a more active role of subnational legislators.

It is worth noting that, even if the number of MPs using human rights treaties is limited, some specific legislators can nonetheless have an impact. First, we observed that some members of parliament who are specifically committed to human rights or to a cause covered by a treaty (equality, women, or disability rights) play an important role in the process through which cantonal authorities engage with human rights treaties. These particularly committed parliamentarians participate in placing the implementation of the treaties, or of specific obligations, on the cantonal political agenda. They can also use the treaties to relay the claims of civil society actors, social movements, or people concerned by the treaties. Second, members of parliaments can also acquire more leverage as they become involved in committees working on legislative proposals and reforms that lead them to work with the treaties and on their implementation. In doing so, they become aware of the treaty and participate in defining an engagement through their amendments or by requesting the government to take measures.

6.1.3 *Engagement of Political Authorities with Human Rights Treaties*

Our study identified three different types of engagement of subnational political authorities with human rights treaties, by which political authorities aim at ensuring their legislative and practical implementation. These types of engagement sometimes follow directly from the uses of the treaties by other actors, such as individual bureaucrats or civil society. As such, they include those that directly aim to implement the treaty, prepare for implementation or comply with specific obligations. In addition, there is a type of embedded engagement, where the treaty or specific parts thereof are used to support a policy change or legislative reform whose main goals are not to implement the treaty and that concern a domain close or related to the treaty. Conversely, uses that do not lead to engagement involve placing the issue of treaty implementation on the political agenda without resulting in any tangible change. Engaging with human rights treaties requires a comprehensive approach that involves enacting laws, making reforms, establishing new rights, allocating budgets and developing action plans. When public policy aligns with the treaty's approach, engagement with the treaty reinforces and legitimises existing efforts and measures, providing opportunities for advancement and evolution. In cantons where the treaty requires significant changes, the treaty creates a window of opportunity to start changing the policy paradigm and take a new policy path. Initiating engagement involves institutionalisation and the impulsion of a new public policy, establishing a new institutional framework and empowering new actors through the creation of new bureaucratic positions or even new offices, in cantons where there were only few (or almost no) concrete and unified public policy in the domain concerned by the treaty. Issue-specific engagement concerns specific obligations of the treaty, which can be part of a broader engagement with the treaty or involve going further with an obligation. Embedded engagement occurs in cantons with well-developed public policies in the domain of the treaty, where policy bureaucrats or members of cantonal parliament can use the treaty or specific obligations as arguments and take measures that can be related to the treaty and that are embedded in a broader project that does not mainly aim at implementing the treaty.

Finally, uses not leading to engagement occur in cantons where the issue of treaty implementation is put on the political agenda but no concrete measures are taken. This can be due to various conditions, including the weakness of political parties supporting the issues under consideration in the cantonal parliament and government (especially left-wing ones in the field of human rights law), an unfavourable balance of power, an underdeveloped existing policy, weak financial resources and no specialised bureaucracy. Small, rural cantons are likely to find themselves in such situations, albeit not exclusively. These structural limitations can be at least partially overcome, however, when the federal level takes its role of providing guidance seriously, and cantonal institutions consequently work under the shadow of the hierarchy (Héritier & Lehmkuhl, 2008), and even more so when small cantons can rely on their counterparts within platforms aiming to structure and organise co-operative horizontal interactions, such as intergovernmental cantonal conferences (Behnke & Mueller, 2017; Schnabel & Mueller, 2017). In these venues, mutual learning processes might occur, facilitating the implementation of complex procedures, while also allowing actors to create new coalitions that may be instrumental for confronting local political opposition.

6.2 Main Implications

To conduct our inquiry, we relied on a systematic case study methodology based on document analysis and in-depth semi-directive interviews with different types of actors on the two investigated treaties: The Council of Europe Convention on Preventing and Combating Violence against Women and Domestic Violence, better known as the Istanbul Convention (IC); and the United Nations Convention on the Rights of Persons with Disabilities (CRPD). Our analytical approach is context-sensitive, insofar as it focuses on the micro-level determinants of the observed regularities and variations in the preferences, behaviour, and consequent aggregate outputs (Coleman, 1994). Specifically, we look at the implications of how local actors use human rights treaties for the engagement of cantonal political authorities with these treaties. This research strategy allowed us to generate a fine-grained understanding of the processes at work and of the perceptions of the relevant actors therein. However, following this approach, the external validity and the limits to the generalisability of our results require special attention. In particular, it is worth discussing the scope conditions under which our main findings are expected to hold. Scope conditions neither explain nor determine the phenomenon under investigation, but they restrict the applicability of a complex causal relation and define the conditions for observing a given result. More specifically, they can provide evidence about relevant contextual variables, and thereby offer an instrument to delimit the context in which hypotheses apply (Falleti & Lynch, 2009; Foschi, 1997; Maggetti, 2015).

Against this background, a number of factors can be distilled from our research, which could possibly work as scope conditions. As scope conditions typically consist of structural elements that shape (but do not fully determine) political actors' identities, perceptions, goals and orientations, and, ultimately, their actions (Scharpf, 2000), we purposively focus on three institutional factors. The first condition allowing subnational actors to make their own use of international treaties is the existence of a certain *room for manoeuvre* at the local level. Such a room for manoeuvre derives from both the autonomous political authority attributed to the federated states and the distance of actors from the central government. Second, the international treaty under consideration needs to imply—as is typically the case—*flexibility* in implementation. A flexible approach to implementation involves the attribution of more leeway to actors targeted by the rules and to those in charge of their implementation in adapting to the local context and to their own preferences, i.e. subsidiarity, for instance by setting objectives rather than strict rules, offering alternative options, allowing for a margin of appreciation of the relevant actors (Treib et al., 2007). The third condition is the presence of *issue-specific* policy competencies, involving political actors—usually, specialised policy bureaucrats—who are entrusted with specific tasks in the areas potentially related to the treaty. The attribution of these tasks allows these actors to claim issue ownership and to develop a credible expertise in the issue area, leading to the emergence of an epistemic community (Niederhauser & Maggetti, 2023).

Under these conditions, as observed in the Swiss case with respect to the two examined human rights treaties, a small number of policy entrepreneurs—possessing specific expertise and with a high intensity of preferences—located at the subnational level are key in triggering purposive uses of the international treaties and thus favouring the engagement of the political authorities of the subnational unit. In turn, their effectiveness is affected by the presence of political coalitions that support or oppose the proposed reforms.

The three above-mentioned institutional factors correspond to some of the main defining features of multilevel polities. This implies that we can possibly extend our findings to other multilevel democratic systems, where background factors are, broadly speaking, comparable, namely when subnational human rights implementation is at stake in other federal democratic states or devolved jurisdictions. For instance, similar dynamics are possibly observable in the United States, where federal institutions largely delegate to states the duty to conform their practices with human rights treaties, and states are keen to retain responsibility over areas that fall under their control. While this situation enables the development of bottom-up, contextual solutions, it is also creating an uneven situation across the country, with some of them falling short of international obligations (Spiro, 1997).

6.3 Looking Forward

Our research points to some blind spots that deserve further attention.

First, while our research has focused on the relationship between rule-makers (governments interacting at the international level) and rule-takers (or targets, at the subnational levels), and specifically on the role of various actors who play an intermediation function (Abbott et al., 2017; also see: Pélisse 2019; Talesh & Pélisse, 2019), rule beneficiaries, i.e. the individuals who are supposed to benefit from increased protection, need to be considered more explicitly. In particular, it would be important to examine how the various uses of treaties and forms of engagement at the subnational level have an impact on the prospected rule beneficiaries. In that regard, it is possible to expect that different uses and different patterns of engagement are associated with different outcomes. For instance, one could assume that when the engagement of political authorities involves a significant bottom-up component, it will more accurately account for the real situation on the ground and therefore be more effective, and the allocation of human and financial resources more sustained. Moreover, it would be particularly relevant to question how international human rights treaties impact the legal consciousness (Chua, 2019; Ewick & Silbey, 1998; Sarat, 1990) of the people concerned (e.g. persons with disabilities, victims of violence against women or domestic violence), especially their rights consciousness (Merry, 2003). The CRPD, for example, seems to have changed the perception certain persons with disabilities conceived the rights they have (and they can claim) and what policy change they can claim for. Besides, this questioning on international law consciousness could be extended to activists and civil society actors to examine how treaties potentially change the way they frame their cause, their claims, their strategies, and their actions.

Second, we did examine implementation processes, especially from the perspective of legislative implementation, but the street-level dimension of implementation has not been directly tackled in our study (Buffat et al., 2016; Lipsky, 2010). However, other actors that hold less institutionalised positions than policy bureaucrats and legislators are also likely to be influential at that level and thereby deserve attention. For instance, studying the day-to-day practices of frontline actors such as social workers would be crucial to examine the extent to which positive obligations derived from the treaties become enshrined into local contexts. Furthermore, it is important to look at the impact of non-institutional practices. As a matter of fact, civil society actors—such as NGOs, charities, and foundations—may draft guidelines inspired by and/or referring to international treaties, which are diffused through more or less formalised channels to directly target street-level actors, such as teachers and police officers, possibly affecting their behaviour.

Third, as soon as local political authorities engage with an international treaty, the latter become institutionalised, and therefore likely to deploy long-term effects on subnational policy processes. As such, a human rights treaty can have a gradual but transformative impact on public policies in the related areas. This type of policy change can occur especially through regulatory layering, corresponding to a process by which the incremental adoption of new rules and the related organisational developments, e.g. the creation of specialised offices in the public administration, eventually alter the logic of the regulatory framework (Maggetti, 2014). This implies that even changes that appear marginal and almost irrelevant in the short term can significantly modify the situation on the ground in the medium-long term. International human rights law thus matters: the accumulation of small changes over time and the degree of coherence of the trajectory of reform could indeed induce a paradigmatic shift in the way the issues at stake are dealt with by the relevant local policy communities. Therefore, such trajectories would also need to be studied in a comprehensive, integrated way, accounting for their historical evolution.

REFERENCES

Abbott, K. W., Levi-Faur, D., & Snidal, D. (2017). Theorizing Regulatory Intermediaries: The RIT Model. *The ANNALS of the American Academy of Political and Social Science, 670*(1), 14–35. https://ssrn.com/abstract=2925411

Behnke, N., & Mueller, S. (2017). The Purpose of Intergovernmental Councils: A Framework for Analysis and Comparison. *Regional & Federal Studies, 27*(5), 507–527.

Benz, A., & Papadopoulos, Y. (2006). Introduction: Governance and Democracy: Concepts and Key Issues. In A. Benz & Y. Papadopoulos (Eds.), *Governance and Democracy* (pp. 1–26). Routledge.

Buffat, A., Hill, M., & Hupe, P. (Eds.). (2016). *Understanding Street-Level Bureaucracy*. Policy Press.

Chua, L., & Engel, D. (2019). Legal Consciousness Reconsidered. *Annual Review of Law and Social Science, 15*, 335–354.

Coleman, J. S. (1994). *Foundations of Social Theory*. Harvard University Press.

Di Capua, R., Pilotti, A., Mach, A., & Lasseb, K. (2022). Political Professionalization and Transformations of Political Career Patterns in Multi-Level States: The Case of Switzerland. *Regional & Federal Studies, 32*(1), 95–114.

Downs, W. (2014). Sub-National Legislatures. In S. Martin, T. Saalfield, & K. Strøm (Eds.), *The Oxford Handbook of Legislative Studies* (pp. 609–627). OUP.

Eberli, D., Bütikofer, S., & Bundi, P. (2019). La professionnalisation dans les parlements cantonaux. In A. Pilotti & O. Mazzoleni (Eds.), *Le système de milice et la professionnalisation politique en Suisse* (pp. 91–126). Livreo-Alphil.

Ewick, P., & Silbey, S. (1998). *The Common Place of Law: Stories from Everyday Life*. University of Chicago Press.

Falleti, T. G., & Lynch, J. F. (2009). Context and Causal Mechanisms in Political Analysis. *Comparative Political Studies, 42*(9), 1143–1166.

Foschi, M. (1997). On Scope Conditions. *Small Group Research, 28*(4), 535–555.

Héritier, A., & Lehmkuhl, D. (2008). The Shadow of Hierarchy and New Modes of Governance. *Journal of Public Policy, 28*(1), 1–17.

Jones, B. D., & Baumgartner, F. R. (2005). *The Politics of Attention: How Government Prioritizes Problems*. University of Chicago Press.

Kingdon, J. W. (2014). *Agendas, Alternatives, and Public Policies* (2nd ed., Pearson New International Edition ed.). Pearson.

Lipsky, M. (2010). *Street-Level Bureaucracy: Dilemmas of the Individual in Public Service*. Russel Sage Foundation.

Maggetti, M. (2014). Institutional Change and the Evolution of the Regulatory State: Evidence From the Swiss Case. *International Review of Administrative Sciences, 80*(2), 276–297.

Maggetti, M. (2015). Knowledge Progress in Comparative Politics. In D. Braun & M. Maggetti (Eds.), *Comparative Politics: Theoretical and Methodological Challenges* (pp. 154–185). Edward Elgar Publishing.

Merry, S. (2003). Rights Talk and the Experience of Law: Implementing Women's Human Rights to Protection from Violence. *Human Rights Quarterly, 25*(2), 343–381.

Mintrom, M., & Norman, P. (2009). Policy Entrepreneurship and Policy Change. *Policy Studies Journal, 37*(4), 649–667.

Niederhauser, M., & Maggetti, M. (2023). Multi-Level Implementation of International Law: The Role of Vertical Epistemic Communities. *Swiss Political Science Review, 29*(4), 399–421.

Papadopoulos, Y. (2008). Europeanization? Two Logics of Change of Policy-Making Patterns in Switzerland. *Journal of Comparative Policy Analysis: Research and Practice, 10*(3), 255–278. https://doi.org/10.1080/13597566.2017.1368017

Pélisse, J. (2019). Varieties of Legal Intermediaries: When Non-Legal Professionals Act as Legal Intermediaries. *Studies in Law, Politics and Society, 81*, 101–128.

Sarat, A. (1990). The Law is All Over: Power, Resistance and the Legal Consciousness of the Welfare Poor. *Yale Journal of Law and the Humanities, 2*, 343–379.

Scharpf, F. W. (2000). Institutions in Comparative Policy Research. *Comparative Political Studies, 33*(6–7), 762–790.

Schnabel, J., & Mueller, S. (2017). Vertical Influence or Horizontal Coordination? The Purpose of Intergovernmental Councils in Switzerland. *Regional & Federal Studies, 27*(5), 549–572. https://doi.org/10.1080/13597566.2017.1368017

Sciarini, P. (2015). From Corporatism to Bureaucratic and Partisan Politics: Changes in Decision-Making Processes over Time. In P. Sciarini, M. Fischer, & D. Traber (Eds.), *Political Decision-Making in Switzerland: The Consensus Model Under Pressure* (pp. 24–50). Palgrave MacMillan.

Sciarini, P., & Fischer, M. (2019). Die Position der Regierung in Entscheidungsstrukturen. In A. Ritz, T. Haldemann, & F. Sager (Eds.), *Blackbox Executive*. NZZ Libro.

Spiro, P. J. (1997). The States and International Human Rights. *Fordham Law Review, 66*(2), 567–596.

Talesh, S., & Pélisse, J. (2019). How Legal Intermediaries Facilitate or Inhibit Social Change. *Studies in Law, Politics, and Society, 79*, 111–145.

Treib, O., Bähr, H., & Falkner, G. (2007). Modes of Governance: Towards a Conceptual Clarification. *Journal of European Public Policy, 14*(1), 1–20.

Varone, F., & Giauque, D. (2022). L'administration fédérale. In Y. Papadopoulos, P. Sciarini, A. Vatter, S. Häusermann, & F. Fossati (Eds.), *Handbuch der Schweizer Politik—Manuel de la politique suisse* (pp. 373–402). NZZ Libro.

Open Access This chapter is licensed under the terms of the Creative Commons Attribution 4.0 International License (http://creativecommons.org/licenses/by/4.0/), which permits use, sharing, adaptation, distribution and reproduction in any medium or format, as long as you give appropriate credit to the original author(s) and the source, provide a link to the Creative Commons license and indicate if changes were made.

The images or other third party material in this chapter are included in the chapter's Creative Commons license, unless indicated otherwise in a credit line to the material. If material is not included in the chapter's Creative Commons license and your intended use is not permitted by statutory regulation or exceeds the permitted use, you will need to obtain permission directly from the copyright holder.

Index

A
Aargau, 37, 38
academic experts, 3, 38, 60, 63, 64, 72, 84, 85, 94, 97, 100, 116, 121. *See also* University
action plan, 11, 38, 50, 53, 56, 59, 62–64, 72, 75, 84, 91, 92, 94, 100–104, 107, 108, 110, 113–116, 123
agenda-setting, 71–74, 76, 83, 84, 104
   institutional, 84
   political, 14, 74
Appenzell Ausserrhoden, 37
Appenzell Innerrhoden, 37, 40, 59
authorities, political, 2–8, 11–19, 23–27, 29, 31, 33–36, 39, 41, 48, 68, 72, 78, 82, 85, 90–95, 97, 98, 100, 101, 104, 105, 107, 109–113, 116, 119–121, 123–127

B
Basel-Landschaft, 38, 94
Basel-Stadt, 37, 94, 95, 97, 103
Berne, 53–56, 58–60, 62, 77, 94, 112
BFEG, 54–58, 63
BFEH, 59–61
bias, 34
bottom-up, 3, 15, 18, 26, 28, 58, 61, 63, 122, 125, 126
Bourdieu, Pierre, 81, 83
budgets, 4, 6, 11, 31, 84, 112, 123
bureaucrats/bureaucracy, 2, 3, 8, 12, 26, 27, 29, 36, 60, 64, 65, 69–72, 84, 85, 92, 97, 98, 100–106, 109, 110, 113–116, 122–124, 126

C
cantonal, 3, 4, 7–11, 17, 24–26, 30–32, 36, 38–41, 48, 51–63, 68–80, 82–85, 90–116, 120–124
cantons, 9–11, 16, 30, 33, 34, 36–40, 50–65, 69–72, 74, 75, 77, 79, 81, 82, 91, 92, 94–96, 99, 100, 102–104, 106, 108–113, 116, 123, 124
case studies, 2, 16, 25, 28, 32, 34, 48, 62–65, 83, 91, 109, 113, 124
civil society, 2, 16, 26, 28, 36, 50, 64, 65, 71, 73, 76, 78, 95, 97, 98, 100, 101, 121, 123, 126
civil society organisations (CSOs), 3, 27, 30, 38, 70, 71, 73, 75, 78, 79, 84, 85, 90, 103
cognitive resource, 2, 12, 35, 72, 78, 83, 85, 107, 115, 121
compliance, 4, 5, 11, 13–16, 49, 62, 90, 107, 116
conditions, enabling or hindering engagement, 109, 114
constitutional law, 2, 25, 99
consultation procedure, 51–53, 55, 58

context, 5, 10, 15, 17, 23, 25, 27–30, 33, 35, 41, 52, 69, 80, 85, 102, 104, 110–112, 121, 122, 124–126
Convention, 31, 32, 38, 51, 53–59, 61–64, 73, 105, 106, 120
Convention on the Rights of Persons with Disabilities (CRPD), 3, 23, 27, 29, 32, 33, 36, 38, 40, 48, 58–64, 68, 70, 72, 73, 75–79, 82, 91, 94–100, 103, 110, 113, 116, 120, 124, 126
Council of Europe, 30, 32, 56
Council of Europe Expert Group on Action against Violence against Women and Domestic Violence (GREVIO), 36, 64, 70, 102
courts, 7, 8, 50

D
data, 2, 3, 9, 12, 16, 24, 25, 33–35, 40, 41
disability/disabilities, 3, 12, 19, 23, 27, 28, 32–34, 60, 61, 69–73, 75–77, 82, 94–100, 110, 113, 116, 121, 123, 126
discrimination, 34, 107
domestic violence, 6, 19, 30, 31, 38, 55, 69–72, 74, 76, 79, 81, 82, 92, 93, 101, 103–106, 111, 112, 116, 126
Donald, Alice, 8, 14, 26, 36, 50, 63, 90
duties to protect. *See* positive obligations

E
engagement
  embedded, 17, 91, 107–109, 115, 123, 124
  implementation-centred, 17, 91–98, 100, 101, 103–105, 107–109, 114–116
  initiating, 17, 91, 104–109, 115, 116, 123
  issue-specific, 98, 114, 123
Eslava, Luis, 5
European Convention on Human Rights, 99
expertise, 10, 72, 85, 121, 122, 125
experts, 16, 51, 52, 55, 57, 60, 61, 63, 71, 73, 94–96, 98, 109, 113

F
federal, 2, 3, 9–11, 13, 23, 24, 29, 31, 33, 36, 38, 40, 48, 51, 53, 54, 56, 58, 59, 62–64, 68–70, 75–77, 99, 112, 113, 116, 121, 122, 125
federalism, 10, 55
federal level, 11, 30, 62–64, 99, 112, 121, 124
financial (means), 81
Fribourg, 37, 38

G
generalisation, 11
Geneva, 36, 38–40, 57, 73, 77–82, 99, 100, 107, 108, 110, 112
Glarus, 37, 38, 106, 107
Graubünden, 37, 38
guide, 38, 50, 60, 61, 63

H
harmonisation (btw cantons), 53, 64
Hess-Klein, Caroline, 94, 99

I
implementation, 2–19, 24–27, 29–32, 34–36, 38–40, 48–65, 69–79, 81, 83, 84, 90, 92–95, 98, 101, 102, 105–108, 110–113, 115, 116, 120, 121, 123–126
implementation bodies, 50, 54
incentives, 63
incorporation, 28, 31
information, 4, 15, 17, 32, 36, 40, 41, 53, 56–58, 61–63, 65, 69, 70, 73, 75, 78, 79, 84, 85, 90, 102, 103, 106, 115, 121, 122
intercantonal, 16, 36
intermediaries, 28, 29, 68, 83
intermediation, 25, 28, 29, 126
international courts/tribunals, 8, 14
international responsibility, 9, 68
intersectionality, 34
interviews, 2, 26, 27, 29, 30, 35, 38–41, 60, 61, 74, 110, 111, 124
Istanbul Convention (IC), 3, 17, 23, 29–36, 38, 40, 48, 52–54, 56–59,

INDEX   133

62–64, 68, 70–77, 79–83, 91–93,
99–108, 110–113, 116, 120, 124

J
judges, 83
Jura, 37, 38, 70, 73, 103

K
Kaempfer, Constance, 6, 10, 16, 25, 48,
49, 53, 63–65, 68, 101
Krommendijk, Jasper, 13, 26

L
law reform, 38, 70, 72, 91, 92, 99, 101,
104, 107, 113–115
left-wing, 73, 109, 110, 114, 115, 124
legal intermediaries, 24, 28
legislation, 6, 13, 31, 33, 51, 59–61, 64,
72, 91–95, 99
legitimacy, 10, 81–83, 93, 123
legitimising. *See* legitimacy
Lucerne, 38

M
Maggetti, Martino, 25, 85, 125, 127
mechanisms, 3, 5, 8, 11, 14, 16, 17, 24,
27, 31, 36, 41, 47–53, 58, 60–65,
91, 101, 103, 121
mediation, 71, 101, 102
members of parliament (MPs), 70, 71,
73–76, 78–80, 84, 85, 93, 94, 99,
102, 103, 110, 111, 114, 122, 123
Merry, Sally Engle, 15, 27–29, 68, 126
Miaz, Jonathan, 10, 28, 68, 83, 101
migration, 34
mobilisation, 3, 14, 27, 35, 80, 122
Mobilizing Human Rights, 5
monism, 10, 16
multi-level, 16, 25, 28

N
Neuchâtel, 38, 40, 55, 71, 72, 74–77,
81, 92, 93, 103
New Legal Realism, 24–27
Nidwald, 37, 59

Niederhauser, Matthieu, 85, 125
non-governmental organisation (NGO),
4, 70, 74, 126
norms, 6–8, 10, 11, 15–18, 27, 34, 35,
69, 82

O
Obwald, 37

P
parliament/parliaments, 3, 7–12, 24, 26,
27, 38–40, 50–52, 54, 56, 59,
68–74, 79–81, 83, 90–93, 95–98,
103–105, 107, 109–111, 115, 121,
122, 124
parliamentary services, 111
Pélisse, Jérôme, 28, 29, 68, 83, 126
policy processes, 2, 4, 8–11, 15, 18,
24–27, 30, 35, 36, 39, 41, 51, 53,
68, 69, 83, 85, 90, 113, 121, 122,
127
political science, 2, 24, 25, 29
political will, 10, 63, 110, 113
positive obligations, 6, 7, 126
procedure, 3, 4, 6, 25, 47–52, 54, 59,
62, 64, 68, 120, 124
process-tracing, 26
public policy, 2, 14, 27, 83, 90, 92,
100, 103, 104, 109, 112, 113, 123
public problem, 30, 31, 33, 35, 71, 72,
81, 83, 85, 121

R
racial discrimination, 34
ratification, 3, 30, 36, 40, 47–49,
51–54, 58, 59, 62, 64, 69, 71, 72,
100, 112, 120
research design, 16, 26
resources, financial/economic, 12, 18,
34, 92, 110, 114, 124, 126
right-wing, 40, 111

S
sanctions, 16, 48, 53, 63, 64
Schaffhausen, 38, 70, 77, 104, 105, 109
Schefer, Markus, 60, 61, 95

Schmid, Evelyne, 6, 23–25
Schwyz, 38, 40, 54, 74, 75
Sikkink, Kathryn, 14
Simmons, Beth, 3, 5, 6, 8, 14, 15, 26, 35, 48–50, 52
size of cantons, 39, 57, 68, 103, 104, 106, 110, 112, 114, 115, 124
Social Democratic Party (of Switzerland), 70, 73–81, 94, 97, 99, 106, 111
sociology of law, 2, 25, 26
Solothurn, 37, 38
specialized bureaucrat(s), 69, 72, 83, 93, 98, 122
specialized policy bureaucrats, 30, 68–73, 81, 83–85, 90, 100–104, 109, 112, 113, 121, 122, 125
St. Gallen, 37, 38, 57
street-level, 85, 101, 103, 126
subnational, 2–11, 13–19, 23–26, 28–31, 33–36, 40, 41, 48–53, 55, 58–65, 68–72, 76–78, 81–83, 85, 90, 91, 93, 95, 96, 98, 100–105, 107–113, 116, 119–123, 125–127
  definition, 125
Swiss Conference against Domestic Violence (CSVD), 54–58, 63, 102
Switzerland, 2, 5, 7, 9, 10, 16, 17, 23, 29–34, 36, 39, 40, 48, 51, 52, 54, 55, 59, 62–65, 68, 76, 80, 94, 96, 107

T
Talesh, Shauhin, 27, 28, 68, 83, 126
Thurgau, 37, 38, 54, 59
Ticino, 37, 81

top-down, 3, 15, 17, 24, 26, 58, 63, 64, 120, 122
translation (of law/norms into policy), 15
treaties, 2–19, 23–36, 38, 39, 41, 47–52, 62–65, 68–79, 81–85, 90, 95, 98, 107–110, 112–114, 119–126
turn to the local, 5

U
United Nations Committee on the Rights of Persons with Disabilities (UNCRPD), 36, 59, 70
United Nations (UN), 36, 50
University. *See also* academic experts
Uri, 37

V
Valais, 37, 38, 72, 94–97, 102, 103
Vaud, 38, 59, 101, 102, 112
violations (human rights), 26
violence against women, 28, 30–32, 55, 64, 69, 70, 74, 75, 81, 82, 92, 105, 106, 111, 126

W
widespread scepticisms of human rights, 18
Wyttenbach, Judith, 8–11, 24

Z
Zug, 37
Zurich, 38, 40, 74, 75, 77, 99, 101–103, 112

SPRINGER NATURE

GPSR Compliance

The European Union's (EU) General Product Safety Regulation (GPSR) is a set of rules that requires consumer products to be safe and our obligations to ensure this.

If you have any concerns about our products, you can contact us on ProductSafety@springernature.com

In case Publisher is established outside the EU, the EU authorized representative is:

Springer Nature Customer Service Center GmbH
Europaplatz 3
69115 Heidelberg, Germany

The manufacturer's authorised representative in the EU is Springer Nature Customer Service Centre GmbH, Europaplatz 3, 69115 Heidelberg, Germany. If you have any concerns regarding our products, please contact ProductSafety@springernature.com

Printed and bound by CPI Group (UK) Ltd, Croydon, CR0 4YY

25/03/2026

02078179-0020